LA… N

an autumn tour of the parks, public places, and history of the lake erie shore

photography & narrative by

JIM MOLLENKOPF

Lake Erie Sojourn

an autumn tour of the parks, public places, and history of the lake erie shore

photography & narrative by

Jim Mollenkopf

P.O. Box 351454, Toledo, Ohio, 43635-1454

ISBN 0-9665910-0-3
Library of Congress Catalog Card Number 98-67389

DEDICATION:

To my father

Contents:

List of Illustrations & Photographs

Map of the Lake Erie Shore

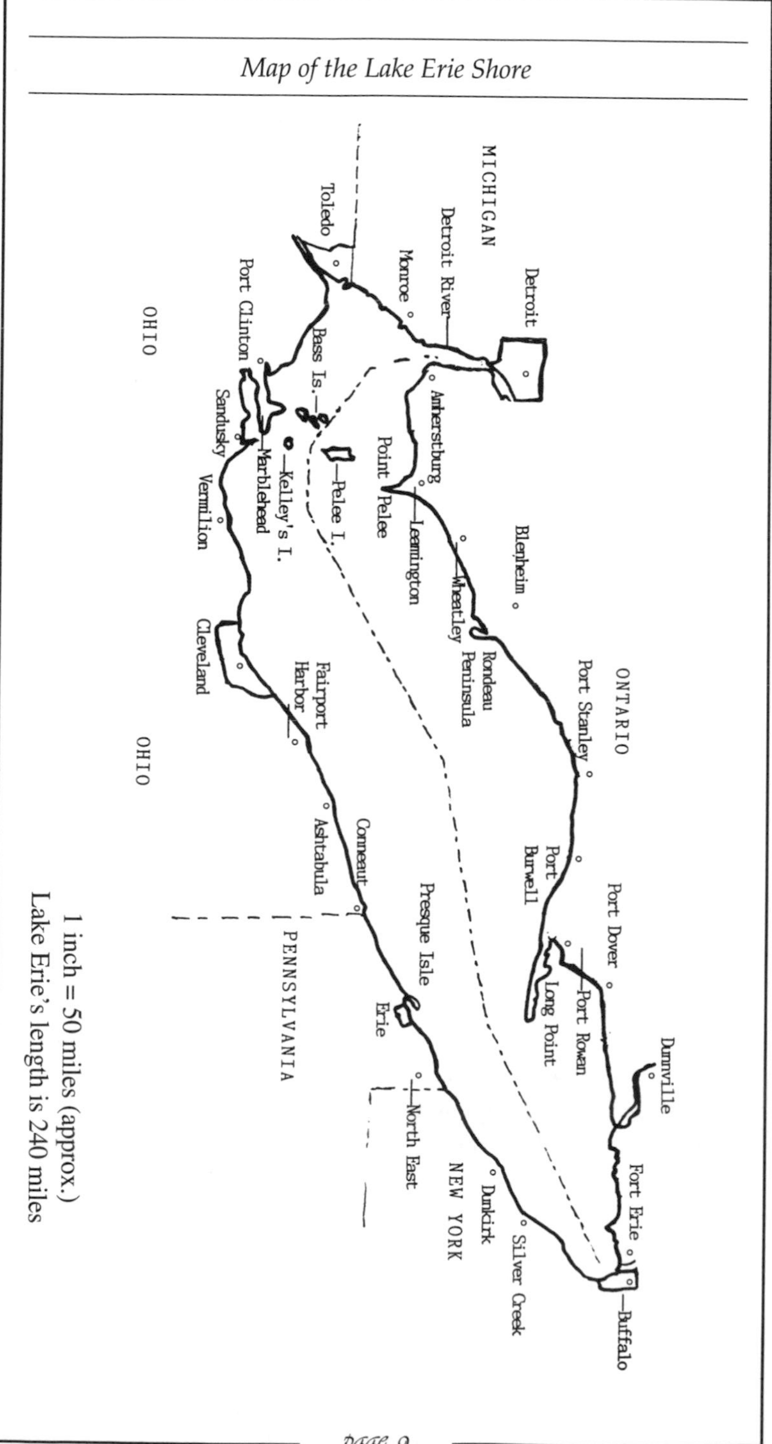

Prologue

Slowly but relentlessly they came. Massive sheets of ice descended to the Midwest in millennia past scraping and gouging the land as they came and melting as they retreated. Their last invasion, about 10,000 years ago, gave final form to that immense repository of fresh water known as the Great Lakes. The southernmost of these is Lake Erie.

Lac du Chat or Lake of the Cat was the name given to Lake Erie on the maps of the earliest French explorers. And the refracted lens of history provides several views as to why.

This was perhaps due to the Eriez Nation of Indians living along the lake and their preference for wearing animal skins. Or it could have been due to the large number of wildcats the French observed prowling near the shore. Or it may have been the Eriez themselves who so named it because, much like a cat, the waters of Lake Erie can be so unpredictable.

In 1655 the relatively peaceful Eriez were destroyed by the fierce Iroquois Confederation from the New York area but Lake Erie's name preserves their legacy. The Iroquois kept the white man at bay for over 100 years, thus Lake Erie was the last of the five Great Lakes to be fully explored and settled by the Europeans.

From Lake Erie's beginning where the Detroit River quietly feeds in the waters of the Upper Great Lakes to its churning exit down the Niagara River in its rush toward Niagara Falls, it is a lake of contrasts.

The Canadian side sleeps in quiet villages and pretty port

towns where fishing boats chug out of misty morning harbors and farmers till lakeside fields. Fort Erie, with a population of 25,000, is by far the largest north shore city. Solitude on the Canadian side is something that can be easily found.

The American side is much more urban and crowded with the industrial cities of Toledo and Buffalo marking its west and east ends respectively and the Cleveland metropolitan area dominating the center. The population of the latter exceeds many times over the combined population of all north communities. Solitude can be also be found on the south shore but only in select areas.

Around the roughly 500 miles of Lake Erie shore can be found soaring cliffs and flat wetlands, marinas bulging with boats and remote fishing piers, shorelines of granite and beaches of sugar sand, and architectural wonders shaped by both human hands and by the forces of nature.

Lake Erie carries the distinctly unglamorous heritage of being the lake that "died." The lake was never actually dead but by around 1965 over a century of pollution had put it in critical condition.

The dumping of nutrient pollutants led to explosive growths of algae which choked much of the oxygen right out of the lake, particularly at the deeper levels where the desirable fish species lived. Walleye, blue pike, and whitefish were replaced by carp, gizzard shad, and sheepshead. The commercial fishing industry collapsed and recreational anglers dropped their lines elsewhere.

Added to this was the sensory effect of scummy masses of floating algae that coated beaches, the discoloration and odors caused by oils and industrial wastes flowing into the lake, and the bacterial pollution that scared away swimmers. And by 1965 Lake Erie looked like it was ready for last rites. Its very name became a term synonymous with environmental tragedy and raw material for comedians; the American Dead Sea.

With nowhere to go but up, embarrassed governments on both sides of the lake were jolted into action to stop the assault on this inland sweetwater sea. A series of legislative mandates were passed in the late 1960's and early 1970's in the atmosphere of a growing environmental movement and the lake began a dramatic turnaround.

As the health of the lake gradually returned so did the schools of sportfish, in particular the walleye. In 1986 4.5 million of them were caught by Ohio anglers, or 45 times the number taken in 1975. But the blue pike will probably never return. And chemical and heavy metal pollution from industry and bacterial pollution from aging urban sewer systems in Lake Erie cities remain as challenges to be met.

The shallowest of the Great Lakes with an average depth of 100 feet Lake Erie can flush itself out in only three years, a capacity that hastened its relatively rapid turnaround. Its enormous cousin Lake Superior needs nearly two centuries to do this. This shallowness also makes it a moody lake as a rising gale can quickly plunge its placid waters into deadly torment, an event that sent many ships to the Lake Erie bottom in the days before modern navigation. The lake's lack of depth allows it to warm in the summer providing excellent swimming at its miles of beaches. Conversely, it usually freezes over in the winter and ice shanty villages of fishermen sprout along the shore. At around 240 miles long and nearly 57 miles wide at its widest point, Lake Erie is the 13th largest body of freshwater in the world.

This book is a descriptive account of an October journey around the immediate shore of Lake Erie, its scenery and quiet places as well as its cities, against the backdrop of the most colorful month of the season. As much as possible at all times on this journey the road closest to the shore was traveled, that being a two-lane township or county road or a multi-lane interstate. The text includes specific road names and directions including jogs through Buffalo, Cleveland, and Toledo.

The large majority of the Lake Erie coast is privately owned. Thus one of the purposes of the book was to find and record the public places where no "keep out" or "no trespassing" signs would hang, places where those without access to a cottage or private development are welcome.

A secondary purpose of the book was to record Lake Erie historical sites and relate historical lore including that of the War of 1812 in which the lake served as a major theater. This was the only time the cannon's roar echoed over the lake, a very bloody war most historians agree should have been fought at the negotiating table.

While this text does not claim to be comprehensive, it does give at least some mention of the vast majority of public places on the lake. The text also provides information on Lake Erie's state and provincial parks and sites of interest along the lakeshore's road and in cities and towns. Some of the parks and tourist sites were closed for the season making only a passing reference possible.

The journey around the lake began in the historic town of Amherstburg, Ontario where the Detroit River meets Lake Erie the first week of October, 1996. It ended at the mouth of the Detroit River on the Michigan shore across from Amherstburg in early November in what was at times a rainy and cool month.

Author's Note: The romantic thing for me to say would be that this book grew out of a lifelong love affair with Lake Erie. It didn't. Having grown up in Cleveland in the 1950's and 1960's and witnessed its demise I, like many people, was disdainful of Lake Erie and vacationed over the years on Lakes Michigan, Superior, and Huron instead. My Lake Erie experience was restricted to grainy childhood memories of swimming at the beaches east of Cleveland and fishing for perch with my father and brothers from a rowboat before the lake became too polluted.

But years of hearing stories of how much of the lake had improved led me to travel its shores to see what was there. In the process I rediscovered the lake of my childhood and, for the first time, experienced the quiet beauty of its Ontario shore. Despite over 200 years of human trampling she's still one pretty lake, a jewel and a resource that demands wise stewardship.

Chapter I:

AMHERSTBURG TO BLENHEIM

October, 1996

This picturesque town breathes history as it hugs the eastern shore of the Detroit River where its swift, blue currents widen and yawn into Lake Erie. The British settled here two hundred years ago building Fort Amhertsburg hard on a bluff of the river and the King's Navy Yard nearby to protect its interest in its Canadian colonies. The Crown also wanted to keep a military eye on that brash young country called the United States of America on the far bank of the river. When tensions between the two countries exploded in the War of 1812, the fort became the British center of operations for the Western Lake Erie theater. Fighting with the British was a confederation of Native-American tribes from the Ohio and Indiana areas united by the oratory and leadership of the legendary Shawnee chief Tecumseh.

The British promised the Natives land if they won the war, territory that was rapidly being devoured by white settlers. And Tecumseh knew this was his last and best chance to hold on to any sort of homelands for his people.

After some early successes, the tide turned against the British and on September 10, 1813 a British naval fleet sailed from Amherstburg to be shattered by American warships in the Battle of Lake Erie. Not bothering to share this information with their Indian allies, the British quietly prepared to retreat. When Tecumseh learned of this, the saddened warrior gave his final recorded speech to the British on September 14.

"Our fleet has gone out, we know they have fought. We have heard the great guns, but know nothing of what has happened...We are much astonished to see our father (the British) tying up everything and preparing to run without letting his red children know what his intentions are...Our lives are in the hands of the Great Spirit. We are determined to defend our lands and if it is his will, we wish to leave our bones upon them."

The British and Indians retreated inland and three weeks later at the Battle of Thames north of here were crushed by a pursuing American army. Tecumseh left his bones upon the land there just as he had prophesied. The Americans occupied the ruins of the fort and were still rebuilding it when the war ended. The British came back in the summer of 1815 and continued the rebuilding and renamed it Fort Malden. By 1851, the last British soldiers left and in succeeding years it became a home for retired soldiers, an insane asylum, and later private residences before being restored as a fort, commemorating a time when war fired Canada's destiny. Fort Malden's grounds can now be walked again. The ghosts of British soldiers far from home or of a solemn Tecumseh heavy with the knowledge his days and those of his beloved people were dwindling can almost be seen in the shadows of the deep earthworks.

In addition to Fort Malden, downtown Amherstburg is also home to historic Old Towne. The backbone this area is Dalhousie Street laid by British soldiers in 1796. Along the Old World ambiance of this avenue can be found The Gordon House, built in 1798, by a Scottish merchant. After laying vacant for a number of years, the city of Amherstburg completed a restoration of the three-story structure in 1996.

The building is leased to a nonprofit group, The H.M.S. Detroit Project, which operates a tea room, gift shop and gallery, and marine exhibit. The group takes its name from the flagship of the British fleet built in Amherstburg during the War of 1812 and plans to build a full-size replica of the warship.

"The Detroit was sunk when we lost the Battle of Lake Erie," the man behind he counter in the gift shop explained from his Canadian perspective. "Later it was refloated and was around until the 1840's when it was sailed down the Niagara River and to the falls in some sort of political protest. From what I understand it was covered with graffiti. Anyway it got stuck on the edge of the falls and was there nearly two years before it finally went over," he added.

Throughout the Gordon House antiques and Georgian style decorating recall the days when the King's men stopped to chat or make a purchase. The marine exhibit tells a story of Amherstburg's naval times and a third story porch offers a sweeping view of Navy Yard Park and the Detroit River.

Navy Yard Park stretches along the river where big lake freighters steam by to Northern ports of call. A pair of ship's cannons, made in 1803 and 1807 respectively, point toward the water. Brick walkways wind around autumn gold trees and manicured beds of flowers, a riot of color even on a cold and wet October day.

Leaving town east on Dalhousie Street is Belle Vue, a sprawling home considered to be the finest remaining example of domestic Georgian architecture in Ontario. Finished in 1819, the riverside home was built by an officer at Fort Malden. The building is now St. Nicholas Ukrainian Catholic Church.

The residents of Amherstburg celebrated their historic town's Bicentennial in 1996, a town which boasts of 35 architecturally historical buildings. Fort Malden, with its 12-acre riverfront site, original earthworks, restored barracks and military reenactments is open for tours daily May 1 through Dec. 24. For other times or more information call 519-736-5416. Amherstburg is also home to The North American Black Historical Museum which records the history of African-Canadians, many who escaped from slavery in America to Canada via the Underground Railroad. Other historical sites include the Gibson Gallery housed in an old railroad depot and the Park House Museum. Amherstburg is also home to a winery which marks the beginning of Southwestern Ontario Wine Trail and hosts a number and of events and festival throughout the year. For more information, contact the Amherstburg Chamber of Commerce at 519-736-2001.

Dalhousie St. leaves Amherstburg and joins provincial highway Ontario 18. Canada's British roots manifest themselves in many ways throughout the country and the declaration "The King's Highway" on Ontario's provincial highway signs is one of them.

East on 18 is the village of Malden Centre. Here CR 50 goes south toward Lake Erie and to the Holiday Beach Conservation Area, a mecca for raptor fans. "Don't miss the annual air show Sept. 1 to mid-December," a sign at the entrance advises and a three-story hawk tower provides the view.

Vultures, osprey, eagles, and huge numbers of hawks obeying their genetic commands to fly south pass through here before the Canadian winter pours in from the north. The hawk migration peaks in September and on September 19, 1984, 96,000 of them passed over Holiday Beach including an astounding 56,000 hawks recorded in an 18 minute period.

Cold and rain have kept most watchers away this day although the hawk tower is host to a few hardy souls as turkey vultures with their magnificent wing span soar overhead. "It's slow now but that could change real quick," advises a man from Windsor who said he'd been a hawk watcher for over 20 years. "It goes in streaks, you know."

He went on to talk about the "busy days" when hawks migrate through in large numbers. "You should see them," he said, "thousands of them, they're everywhere. I get lost watching them. Sometimes I look at my watch and four or five hours slipped by and I hardly realized it."

Holiday Beach Conservation Area offers camping, swimming, a stocked trout pond, and is considered to be one of the premier hawk migration observation points in North America with hawk festivals in September and October. For more information, call 519-736-3772.

Just east of Holiday Beach is the Essex County Demonstration Farm, a joint private/public venture that demonstrates new farming technologies such as no-till farming, use of municipal sludge on cropland, windbreaks for erosion control, and use of wetlands and grasslands as buffers.

CR 50 continues east along the lake to the hamlet of Colchester. A right on Jackson St. leads to a town park sitting on a bluff with a marina and public beach below. The old graveyard of Christ Church Cemetery lies to the east on the same bluff, the resting place of many of the first settlers to the area. Some of the old stones have fallen over. Others slant toward the sky at odd angles.

At the edge of the graveyard near the lake a rusting steel plate bolted to one of the stones bears the pain and faith of a grieving young husband. "Sacred to the memory is Maria Swanston, for one short year the beloved wife of William Duff Esq. of Chestnut Grove. Died at Chippawa in the County of Welland Sept. 27 1854 aged 27 Yrs. I know that my redeemer lives." A small stone building in the cemetery serves as the church's chapel. A replica of the first church built by settlers here, it was originally built in 1819 and rebuilt in 1957. A key is available at the rectory across the street.

Continuing east on CR 50 is the village of Oxley and the John R. Park Homestead and Conservation Area. Park came to this wilderness from Massachusetts in the 1820's and built a 114-acre farm and business hard on the Erie shore. A dozen buildings remain including his 1842 Greek Revival home, its green shuttered exterior facing the lake.

Only the gentle slapping of the waves on the rocky shore below the front porch can be heard this gray day as a distant freighter trails smoke into the mist. Perhaps Park would pause on this porch after a hard days work to admire the wind-filled sails of a merchant ship as it hurried by his north shore home and on to ports of call.

The John R. Park Homestead includes preserved and restored buildings, a gift shop and visitor center, and hosts special events the year-round. For more information, call 519-738-2029.

East of Oxley on CR 50 is the Cedar Creek Conservation Area, a day-use park in Cedar Beach. Here the rocky shore turns into a broad, sandy beach ideal for swimming. Continuing east are the villages of Cedarhurst and Linden Beach, the shores of which are lined shoulder-to-shoulder with cottages, most battened down for the winter.

CR 50 now swings north and rejoins Ontario 18 at the town of Kingsville. Downtown Kingsville bustles, its Victorian brick buildings in good repair and thriving with commerce. Division Street heads south to the lake where the rolling Lakeside Park is home to an historic green and white shelter house overlooking the lake. The large park has trails, tables, and a beach while gardens and gazebos are being added. At the edge of Kingsville grapevines growing along a parking lot mark the Pelee Island Winery. More grapes dangling from an overhead trestle escort visitors inside where the grapes of Pelee Island are transformed from raw fruit to fine wine. Tours of the winery end in a tasting room, its wine cellar ambiance host to several dozen tasters from a charter bus this day. With a steady rain falling outside, they are in no hurry to leave.

Several miles northwest of Kingsville is the Jack Miner Bird Sanctuary, established in 1904 by the man called the "Father of Canadian Conservation." Born near Cleveland in 1865, Miner's family moved to Kingsville when he was 13 where Jack became a hunter of renown.

He became intrigued by the ability of Canada geese to recognize him as an enemy and wondered if he could convert them into recognizing him as a friend. So in 1904 be dug a pond on his small farm, stocked it with pet geese, put out food, and waited.

After several years with no success a few migrating geese landed at his farm in 1908. When they returned the following year bringing more geese with them Miner knew he had established a sanctuary. He spent the rest of his life expanding and developing the haven that now bears his name.

Now clouds of Canada geese and many varieties of ducks flock here during spring and fall migration. There's a museum, nature stadium, and pond area where waterfowl can be hand fed. Over 200,000 waterfowl have been tagged here since 1909 and admission to the grounds has always been free. "Let there be one place on earth where no money changes hands," Jack Miner said before he died in 1944.

The Jack Miner Sanctuary is on CR 23 northwest of Kingsville and is open daily, closed on Sundays. Best viewing times are the last two weeks of October and all of November and the last two weeks in March and the first week in April. School groups by appointment only. For more information call 519-733-0404.

Leaving Kingsville, Ontario 18 goes inland and the road becomes CR 20 as it heads toward Leamington. Southwest Ontario has been called the "breadbasket of the province," a fact much in evidence along this road. Prosperous farms abound, their harvests still being gathered from the fields. Apples, pumpkins, tomatoes, and squash make the frequent produce stands a cornucopia of color.

At the edge of Leamington, Seacliff Park slopes from the road, the picnic area darkened by stands of mature oaks and maples. Where the park meets the lake is a sizable swimming beach.

Adjacent to the park, Erie Street heads south to Leamington Harbor and marina which has undergone an extensive renovation. Brick walkways, gardens, and ornate lampposts brighten this place even on a dreary day. The ferry M. V. Pelee Islander rocks gently at her dock, its parking lot empty, a meeting place for hundreds of gulls grounded by the weather. Going north on Erie Street gives entry into the city that claims the title of "Tomato Capital of Canada" and the smell of simmering tomatoes from the sprawling Heinz processing plant gives credence to that claim. At the intersection of West Talbot and Mill Streets in Leamington's busy downtown shopping district is the tourist information booth shaped, like what else, a tomato.

CR 33 leaves south from Leamington to the birder's shrine of Point Pelee National Park. This southernmost point of mainland Canada swarms with warblers during spring migration and fills with legions of monarch butterflies and raptors in the fall. Observation towers, floating boardwalks, and canoes give the marsh lover the chance to explore the diversity of life nourished in the wetlands of this sandy point. The value of Pelee was confirmed in 1918 when it became the first national park so designated for its ecological importance rather than tourism potential.

A light rain falls from the sky this gray day giving rise to a melodious hiss from the still waters below the Marsh Boardwalk. A number of birdwatchers in colorful raincoats move along alone or in small groups speaking in hushed tones as if at a museum. Several hawks, their silhouettes etched against an ashen sky, soar overhead in search of sustenance to carry them on their journey south.

Leamington provides a jumping-off point for two popular visitor destinations in Southern Ontario; Point Pelee National Park and Pelee Island in Lake Erie. The park is a year-round day-use facility with over 500,000 visitors per year. In addition to its natural attractions and nature programs, the park offers swimming, hiking, canoe and bicycle rentals, and cross-country skiing and swamp-skating in the winter. For more information, call the park at 519-322-2365. Pelee Island is a summertime draw for nature lovers to see its rare and endangered bird species and for wine connoisseurs to the seminars, samples, and vineyard tours at the Pelee Island Wine Pavilion. For Pelee Island ferry information, call 800-661-2220.

Leaving the park north on CR 33, CR 20 heads east and zig- zags a bit to the Hillman Marsh Conservation Area on CR 37, another spring bird migration spot and wetland-rich area with walking trails, picnicking, and a nature center open seasonally.

CR 37 goes north and joins Ontario 3. Road signs mark this as "The Talbot Trail" for Thomas Talbot, an early surveyor and land manager to this area. Eastward lies the Kopegaron Woods Conservation Area, a Carolinian Woods hiking trail where a dense forest shadows the earth's floor. Carolinian Woods are hardwood stands typical of those found in the east-central United States. Beyond this is the village of Wheatley, home to the lakeside provincial park of the same name. Shaded sites await campers here and there's a picnic ground on a low, beachside bluff.

The town of Wheatley lays claim to being the "Freshwater Fishing Capital of North America" with a large commercial fishing fleet returning to harbor heavy with catch in the late afternoons and buckets of smelt being scooped from the provincial park's beach in late April and early May. The park's quiet and wooded grounds are bisected by three creeks which are ideal for canoeing. Over 200 sites, some with electrical hookups, are available in three campgrounds with showers/flush toilets. For more information, call Wheatley Provincial Park at 519-825-4659. For town information, call 519-825-3603.

From Wheatley, Ontario 3 obeys the northeast slant of the Lake Erie shore. The lake appears and disappears according to the undulations of the road as it travels through rich farmland. Talbot Street United Church, an old red brick church, sprouts out of the seemingly endless fields along Ontario 3. Its founders laid its cornerstone in 1902.

Continuing down The Talbot Trail, the lake is now a constant companion to the south as the road has edged closer to the shore and travels on a low bluff. Only a few homes and farmhouses are scattered along the road here as corn and soybean fields line the lakeshore.

Just outside Dealtown is the aging white frame building of Christ Church, built in 1868, and now used only for an annual memorial service in June. Through the window can be seen worn wooden pews with prayer books still in place and a brilliant stained glass window above the altar area. Huge red maple trees, easily as old as the church itself, mark the east and west ends of the cemetery surrounding the church. At Cedar Springs, CR 10 or Charing Cross Road provides the opportunity to travel back toward the lake and to Erie Beach, a small community of neat brick homes and cottages.

From Erie Beach, Erie Shore Road stabs out into the lake along a short peninsula. The cottages along here sit perilously close to the level of the lake and are protected by a hodgepodge of breakwalls, many looking as if they were piled in haste. A Southern gale is cause for anxiety here.

Erie Shore Road comes to Erieau Road and a right turn leads to the McGeachy Pond Management Area, a marsh separated from Lake Erie by a stout dike. A 25-foot tall viewing platform atop the dike gives a sweeping view of the area. To the north spread the marshes of McGeachy Pond and rich farmland created from drained wetlands. To the south the lake stretches gray and seamless on this cold and rainy day until it disappears into the low clouds on the horizon.

Erieau Road curves from McGeachy Pond into the village of the same name which is perched at the end of the peninsula. Erieau was once the busiest coal port on the north shore, a fact belied by the quiet of this place. The only road into town splits into a boulevard of cottages. Tall cottonwood trees line the median.

Laverne Kelly Memorial Park provides a good-sized swimming beach backed by low sand dunes. A sizable marina is also here along with some of Ontario's commercial fishing fleet; the Cindy Lou, the Kar-Lou, and the Fan-C-III are a few of the boats quietly awaiting their next journey to the lake's fishing grounds.

A stone's throw across the water where the peninsula ends is the tip of the Rondeau Peninsula, the two points of land creating a narrow strait giving entrance to the sheltered waters of Rondeau Harbor. Surrounded on three sides by water, there's an end of the earth feel here.

The road into Erieau is also the road out which becomes CR 12 and travels away from the lake and back to Ontario 3 and Blenheim. The neat brick buildings, busy downtown area, and well-kept homes and old churches of Blenheim are typical of the Canadian towns found along this north shore.

Chapter II:

Blenheim to Long Point

As Ontario 3 leaves Blenheim to the south, there's an elaborate gate on the grounds of Blenheim Memorial Park and a marker that tells of McKee's Purchase, a 1790 treaty with four Indian tribes that opened up Southwest Ontario to British and Loyalist settlement.

Ontario 3 continues south briefly before turning to the east. On the right, CR 11 goes south toward the lake and to Shrewsbury, a collection of homes and cottages not quite on the lake but remote and quiet.

CR 11 (New Scotland Road) becomes eastbound at Shrewsbury and passes by one fine old brick home after another. A farmer, discing his rich lowland field under a rising morning sun, is trailed by an army of sea gulls feeding on the bounty of food unearthed by his blades. At the intersection with Ontario 51 is New Scotland, or what's left of it. Only a church with an 1879 cornerstone and a cafe with a "closed" sign in the window are here. If there was a town here at one time it's gone now.

Ontario 51 heads for the lake where it ends at the cottage community of Rondeau Park, gateway to Rondeau Provincial Park. This peninsula park, the second oldest in Ontario, is a blend of flora and fauna, wetland and open lake, and is home to the largest southern hardwood forest in Ontario. Stands of beech, black walnut, tulip, oak, and maple trees line hiking trails here. Like Point Pelee and Holiday Beach, the air here fills with the melodies of songbirds in the spring.

The long, sandy peninsula provides miles of Lake Erie swimming and the opportunity for quiet solitude. Rondeau Bay on the peninsula's inner side was once a refuge for damaged British ships of war where repairs could be made in its calm waters.

French explorers, noting the stand of pine trees sprouting on the tip of the peninsula, named it *Point aux Pins.* The name remains today.

Rondeau Provincial Park offers seasonal camping, sailing and windsurfing opportunities in the natural protection of Rondeau Bay, and is the largest Canadian breeding ground of the beautiful and elusive prothonotary warbler. Fishermen drop lines in the marsh for pike, perch, and bass and bicyclists pedal the 23 kilometers of bike trails and 25 kilometers of park roads. The campground features 258 sites, some with electrical hookups, and showers/flush toilets. For more information, call the park at 519-674-5405.

Eastward from Rondeau Park, CR 17 provides a waterside drive as it grips the edge of the lake. A slice of land squeezed between the road and lake called Kent County Park has a small swimming beach and a picnic ground shaded by sturdy walnut trees. Erosion is trimming away this quiet little park and the roots of beachside trees dangle in the water.

As CR 17 continues its roll along the lake a great flock of ducks, a thousand at least, comes into view floating in the water about 100 yards off shore. The mass rises and falls slightly in Lake Erie's low waves in dark silhouette against the horizon's morning clouds.

A man in a pickup truck stops and informs that the congregation has been in the area about a week, which is unusual. He speculates that the ducks are feeding on a healthy crop of minnows coming into the lake from local streams and that they'll soon resume their migration south.

The road curves away from the lake and Ontario 3 is rejoined at Morpeth. Ontario 3 heads east out town and after a few miles Trinity Anglican Church, built in 1845, crowns a hill on the right. A marker in the quiet churchyard tells of the life of Morpeth native Archibald Lampman who became a poet of renown in the late 19th century.

Born here in 1861, his love of poetry was encouraged by his father who was the rector of the church. He was considered to be one of Canada's leading nature poets but also decried the dehumanization and urbanization caused by the Industrial Revolution.

Archibald Lampman spent most his adult life in Ottawa, a poorly paid postal clerk. A childhood bout of rheumatic fever left him weakened and illness cut his life short in 1899 at the age of 38.

> I see the crowds for ever
> Go by with hurrying feet;
> Through doors that darken never
> I hear the engines beat.
> Through the days and nights that follow
> The hidden mill-wheel strains;
> In the midnight's windy hollow
> I hear the roar of trains...
> Canst thou not rest, O city,
> That liest so wide, so fair;
> Shall never an hour bring pity,
> Nor end be found for care?
>
> From *"The City."*

From the churchyard, Ontario 3 travels parallel to but away from the lake through continuous farmland and eventually rolls through the hamlet of Palmyra. On the east edge of town is an 1880 schoolhouse, now used as a town hall. A plaque here tells the story of a local boy who made good, the Honorable David Mills. He was born on this property and rose through the ranks of the Canadian government to an eventual seat on the Supreme Court before his death in 1903.

The road continues to another area with roots that reach to Scotland, the crossroad of New Glasgow. Here CR 3 goes south to Port Glasgow and ends at the lake and Memorial Park with its large trees and shelter house. A monument gives some history of the town's Scottish beginnings, settlers who landed here in 1813 and carved a community out of virgin forest. A millstone near the monument was first housed in a Port Talbot mill burned to the ground by American forces in 1814. It was then brought to a mill in New Glasgow where it ground grain until the 1890's before becoming part of the foundation of a barn. It's now on display in this quiet park, a stone testament to the area's past.

West of Memorial Park, a road descends to the Port Glasgow Marina. To the west of the marina is a parking lot and a wooden footbridge that spans a river to a small and secluded public beach.

Back onto eastbound Ontario 3 beyond the crossroad of Eagle, McKillop Sideroad dead-ends at the E.M. Warwick Conservation Area, a day-use picnic ground and beach, its gates locked for the winter.

Ontario 3 continues to Wallacetown and CR 8 leads back to the lake and a provincial day-use park and an historic church. John E. Pearce Provincial Park is a winding drive through an almost pure stand of virgin beech trees, a serene woods punctuated by aging and gnarled black locusts. On the forest floor, young beech saplings reach for the light deep in the shadow of their towering ancestral forbears.

A small picnic ground teeters on a cliff 100 feet above the shimmering waters of Lake Erie and gives a spectacular view. Erosion has cleaved into the cliff at the edge of the picnic ground. The roots of a dead tree dangle into the precipice, timber that will soon tumble and crash down to the lake. The face of the clay bluff is peppered with small holes where cliff swallows make their home and a lucky birdwatcher could see a bald eagle soaring by on a current of wind here as it patrols the shore.

St. Peter's Anglican Church of Canada stands sentry outside the gates of the park and its cathedral of trees. The nave of this white structure rose in 1827 while the bell tower was added in 1845 to house a bell donated by the Earl of Galloway, a bell that still calls churchgoers to services. The grounds of this Early Gothic Revival church glow golden from maple leaves falling silently to the earth as this house of worship feels the chill of its 169th autumn.

John Pearce
Provincial Park

Across the lane is the church cemetery. A walking stick carved from a branch of beech leans against the white picket fence fronting this burying ground, there perhaps to help an elderly spouse to the grave of a lost mate. Dedicated "in the memory of all the undaunted pioneers who left home and country to settle on the north shore of Lake Erie," the first marked burial here dates to 1825. Many Pearces are buried here including John Pearce who was born during the American Revolution in Rhode Island in 1777 and came here with his wife Frances, an immigrant from the hills of Ireland. Together they carved lives out of the wilderness of the Lake Erie shore and helped establish the church across the road. Their descendants had the wisdom to preserve the woodlands that now preserve the family name.

Leaving the cemetery, the road becomes a gravel affair briefly called Lakeview Line and journeys east until it intersects with CR 16, a.k.a. Fingal Line. On this road is a monument that tells the tale of Thomas Talbot, sent by the Crown in 1803 to manage the land between Long Point and the Detroit River. Extensive road building and other methods of close, personal control, allowed him to keep out land speculators thus paving the way for hard working and grateful settlers.

His power was the near equal to that of a feudal baron as he granted land to those he deemed worthy and denied it to those he did not. This brought him into conflict with those with differing interests and led to his eventual ouster. His legacy is that of a land transformed from wilderness to productive farms and neat villages and towns.

Down the road on CR 16 is the War to Roses Walking Trail, a now quiet place where once was heard the roar of fighters and bombers at a Royal Canadian Air Force bombing and gunnery school during World War II. A trail with 10 posted stops winds through the grounds of the former base, land being reclaimed by nature with the assistance of local environmental and wildlife groups.

Only the crumbling foundations of the school's buildings remain. Over 130,000 air crew from Canada, the United Kingdom, and the United States were graduated before war's end. A plaque near the trail's entrance lists the names of 19 who died in plane crashes and other accidents here, casualties of a war being fought a half world away.

At Fingal, CR 20 slants back toward the lake. Along the way orchard hands work fast plucking bright red apples from their trees, a forecast of frost lending urgency to their work.

CR 20 begins to descend and before long the postcard-pretty village of Port Stanley spreads before the eyes along the banks of Kettle Creek where it flows into Lake Erie. Here train lovers can ride the rails of history on the Port Stanley Terminal Rail. Originally established as the London to Port Stanley Railway in 1856, it carried over a million passengers a year some years until the Depression and the post-World War II love affair with the automobile brought about its demise. Again a working railway, it now takes passengers on scenic tours of the area countryside.

Port Stanley's harbor has been a lure for travelers since 1832 when ferry service was established from Buffalo. It was considered to be a premier tourist spot on the lake by the 1900's and the shouts of casino gamblers and the sounds of bands such as Guy Lombardo's floated from the renowned Stork Club and into the summer night.

The Stork Club is part of Port Stanley's past but the village remains a recreational and working port, home to a large marina and commercial fishermen who unload their catch to be packed at riverside plants. Ferries no longer call on the deep water harbor but lake freighters dock to transact in coal and grain.

Bridge Street in downtown Port Stanley bustles with restaurants and specialty shops while Main Street on Kettle Creek's east bank boasts of antique and art galleries housed in buildings dating to the 1870's.

On a bright October afternoon the King George VI lift bridge over Kettle Creek raises skyward and downtown strollers stop to admire it and the large sailboat gliding serenely by on its way to Lake Erie. It was far darker day here on December 19, 1937 when a cofferdam collapsed and eight bridge workers lost their lives. The old town hall near the bridge was pressed into service as a temporary morgue.

Port Stanley is home to three swimming beaches, the year-round Port Stanley Terminal Rail, paddle wheel boat rides, and a summer theater and summer festivals, For more information, call the Village Hall at 519-782-3383.

Ontario 4 climbs north out of Port Stanley to CR 23 which quickly leads to CR 24. This road plunges down a hill to the village of Port Bruce where Catfish Creek has carved through the land on its path to Lake Erie. A broad beach for swimming at Port Bruce Provincial Park is here. On Colen Street along Catfish Creek is an 1854 resort hotel with fine first and second story porches, now private residences. Some cottages near the lake, a village park on the creek and some large homes built into the hills above are all else that is here, a peaceful place.

"Catfish," a middle-aged woman fishing on the creek says. "What else do think is in Catfish Creek? I catch 'em, take 'em home, and feed 'em to my cats," she laughs, obviously enjoying herself. On a more serious note she adds "It's so quiet here. Especially now. On weekends in the summer the beach gets a little busy but after Labor Day just about everybody's gone."

Imperial 73 leaves Port Bruce to the north and CR 42 crosses the road at Copenhagen and goes east to Port Burwell as the progression of pretty port towns on this north shore continues. The self-described "Jewel of Lake Erie," Port Burwell clings to the high eastern bank of Big Otter Creek. A vista of Lake Erie and of the long fishing piers that escort the creek into the lake serve as a village backdrop.

An historic lighthouse is here, one of the oldest wooden ones in Canada, its white sides trimmed in red rising nearly 70 feet. Built in 1840, it was rebuilt in 1986 by Mennonite craftsmen using period tools and materials. On a climb up the old wood steps of the lighthouse, the great hewn beams in its walls draw slowly nearer until the last of 60 steps arrives at the apex and the light and a sweeping view of the area. Its been a long time since an oil lamp steered ships from harm's way. But the large, glass lens from France that the light shined through is still here.

Colonel Mahlon Burwell came here in the 1830's to survey the area and in 1836 established the historic Anglican Church and Cemetery where services in three denominations are still held. Another example of Early Gothic Revival architecture, the white steeple of the simple but elegant church reaches toward the heavens above the graves of Port Burwell's earliest residents.

A onetime shipbuilding center that built sailing vessels by the score in the last century, the village and area once boasted of 29 sawmills. Now a provincial park and six private grounds provide ample camping.

Port Burwell Provincial Park features a sandy beach and trails that pass through meadows and woods to high bluffs above. Over 200 campsites are available in three, deeply wooded campgrounds, none with electrical hook-ups, with showers/flush toilets. For park information, call the park at 519-874-4691. The village and area also have private campgrounds and cottage rentals, a marine museum, lighthouse tours, and an historical walking tour. For village information, call 519-874-4343.

From Port Burwell, CR 42 becomes H-N 42 (Haldimand-Norfolk 42) and continues its crawl along the lake while farmers troll their fields in combines collecting their golden harvest of corn and soybeans. The tobacco crop, long since gathered, hangs in the scores of drying barns seen from the road. Local high school students do much of the labor-intensive tobacco picking in September and don't start school until the middle of the month. African-Americans, escaping from slavery in the South, are believed to have established tobacco growing in Ontario. Lake Erie, being the southernmost of the Great Lakes, was a favored crossing point into Canada and an escaped slave could hitch a ride with a friendly boat captain or make a river crossing at Detroit or Buffalo. Around 60,000 to 75,000 slaves had made their way to Canada by the start of the Civil War.

About seven miles east of Port Burwell on H-N 42 is Sand Hill Park, privately owned , but open to the public seasonally. Southwesterly winds off of Lake Erie have been piling sand here for centuries and a mountain of it towers 350 feet over the lake. A mirror on top of the hill was once part of a relay that flashed nautical information across the lake to Pennsylvania. Camping, picnicking, swimming, and some serious dune-

Port Stanley, Ontario

St. Peter's Anglican Church

climbing are available here. The property has been in the same family since 1850.

Sand Hill Park is open May 1st through (Canadian) Thanksgiving. For more information call 519-586-3891.

The Lee Brown Waterfowl Management Area lies beyond Clear Creek on H-N 42, a 280-acre preserve donated by its namesake whose dream was to create and preserve wetlands and create havens for the Canada goose, a bird nearly extinct by 1960 and brought back in great numbers through efforts like this one. A 25-foot high platform gives a view of a pond and waterfowl here. H-N 42, still The Talbot Trail, goes away from the lake for awhile until it meets Ontario 59 which goes south to Long Point, a recreational and naturalist's paradise and one that calls itself "Ontario's best kept secret." Here can be found a sublime present, one preceded by a wild past.

Ontario 59 becomes a willow-lined causeway as it travels to the base of Long Point, an over 20-mile sabre of sand forged on the anvil of wind and lake for thousands of years. Each passing storm plays sculptor to the restless and still growing point. Long Point meant life or death for ships and those who sailed on them in the past when the lake became angry. For those reaching its protective bay on the north, a chance to see the sun rise again while for those caught on its tip or slammed against its southern face and sand bars, a watery death.

Scores of nineteenth century sailors sleep with their ships under the shifting sands in what the men of the sea once called the "Graveyard of the Great Lakes." A grim task of Long Point shore patrolmen once upon a time was to walk the beaches after a mighty gale to look for death's delivery. Man at his worst could once be found on Long Point as brawling camps of lumbermen kept local gendarmes busy and outlaws living in south shore shacks plundered ships and their sailors, leaving behind tales of buried treasure and murder. Poachers working for whiskey were taking a tremendous toll on the point's wildlife and woods by the middle of last century and houses of gambling and prostitution lit the night.

Responding to complaints, the Canadian government sold

the land in 1866 to a group of concerned citizens called the Long Point Company which brought civilization and conservation to the area for the first time since the white man's arrival. Long Point has come a long way since then and its unique habitat has earned it designation as a Biosphere Reserve by the United Nations, one of only 300 in the world. Its quiet marshes and wet meadows are home to thousands of plant and amphibious species, many of them rare or endangered. Over 370 species of birds have been recorded in Long Point with nearly half that number nesting here. And over a half dozen species of turtles march from marsh to sand dune in June to lay their eggs.

At Long Point Provincial Park the shallow waters of the park's beach warm rapidly in the summer providing outstanding swimming. The deep blue water is of a clarity and color normally more associated with Lakes Huron or Michigan than with Lake Erie. The sand, accented in places with red and black by minerals, is piled into great dunes all along the shore.

The beach of Long Point Provincial Park also gives the opportunity to witness the power of lake as sandbars, some only a few feet offshore, are under construction. Each wave rippling over the flat shelf of the bars drops another deposit of sand, a process that continues until a shift in the wind and waves sweeps the bars away and builds new ones elsewhere.

The campgrounds of the park provide a seashore experience. Many sites are perched on, or are sunken into, sand dunes. Some back up to wet areas that provide outstanding birdwatching. Others are cut into stands of red pine while throughout the grounds great cottonwood and aspen trees, some cloaked with thick vines, abound.

Near the park's entrance the Old Cut Lighthouse built in 1879 stands, its lifesaving beam long since dimmed, its weathered green paint peeling in the soft October sun. The cut through which the light once guided ships anxious to avoid the dangers of travel around the point was filled by a furious storm in 1906.

On Old Cut Boulevard beyond the lighthouse is the Long Point Bird Observatory and Visitor Center where staff and volunteers band birds during spring and fall migration. The birds are caught in delicate mist nets placed around the grounds, brought into the center, given a quick examination, banded, and released. Over a half a million birds have been banded since 1960 providing valuable information on migration patterns and on the general health of bird species.

On this day a volunteer gently pulls a Nashville warbler from the cloth bag used to bring birds in from the nets. The tiny bird with a brilliant yellow underbelly and blue-gray head struggles a bit as the volunteer blows softly on his underside to separate his feathers and check for body fat while a small but fascinated audience watches.

The Senior Warden records the information and a little aluminum band is delicately placed around the bird's wisp of an ankle. He is weighed, then released through a trap door, a blur rushing back into the woods and quite eager to leave his human handlers behind.

The Long Point peninsula is accessible to the public up to Long Point Provincial Park as the rest of the peninsula remains privately held. The park has 258 sites, some with electrical hookups, in four campgrounds with showers/flush toilets. Reservations are recommended for midsummer. For more information, call the park at 519-586-2133. The Long Point Bird Observatory's Old Cut Field Station and Visitor Center conducts bird-banding demonstrations mornings from April through mid-June and from mid-August through October. For more information, call 519-586-2885.

Long Point Provincial Park, Ontario

Chapter III:

LONG POINT TO FORT ERIE

Back on CR 42, the road climbs to the village of Port Rowan. Here the blue vista of Inner Bay, created by Long Point's embrace, provides the backdrop on a Main Street stroll. Flotillas of geese and ducks bob on the surface of Inner Bay, its waters and marshy edges known for outstanding bass fishing.

On a hill above the marina near the soldiers and sailors monument, a marker tells the story of Abigail Becker, the "Heroine of Long Point." During a furious November storm in 1854, her husband away, she repeatedly entered freezing Lake Erie waters to assist the exhausted crew of a schooner which had foundered on a sandbar offshore. The sailors were housed and fed in her cabin until they recovered from their ordeal. About a mile east of Port Rowan on CR 42 is the Backus Heritage Conservation Area, a rolling and wooded grounds with over a dozen historic buildings. A grain mill whose foundation was laid 200 years ago is the centerpiece.

The three-story mill was built in 1798 by John Backhouse, a Yorkshire native who came to the United States in 1791 but soon struck out for Canada. On a cold but brilliant blue October morning with dew heavy on the ground, the rush of water down the spillway of the mill is interrupted only by a noisy flock of robins feeding in a crab apple tree before continuing their journey south. The surface of the mill pond is ablaze with the reflection of October gold sugar maples gracing its shore.

Backhouse must have experienced many such mornings here including the one when he heard his country's call and left his peaceful homestead to serve as a major in the Norfolk Militia during the War of 1812. Did he pass through Fort Amherstburg? Did he know Tecumseh? The answers are shrouded in the mists of time.

Major Backhouse returned from the war and, to his relief, found his mill intact. Unlike other north shore mills, it escaped being burned by American soldiers as the valley it sits in hid it from view. It went on to be the longest operating mill in all of Ontario and still grinds grain for visitors today. His descendants, who shortened the family name to Backus, kept the mill until 1955 when it was purchased by the local conservation authority. The conservation area is also home to a 700-acre Carolinian Woods with hiking trails, regarded as the largest such forest in Canada, and an Education Center with excellent displays that tell the area's history and give a peek into Long Point's past. Camping is also available.

In addition to the historic mill, restored buildings in Backus Heritage Conservation Area include a schoolhouse, church, cider press, sawmill, blacksmith shop, and an agricultural museum with historic farm equipment. Family and group camping is available with 160 sites in five campgrounds. For more information, call 519-428-4623.

From the conservation area, CR 42 rolls east to the village of St. Williams. At the four-way stop sign, a right turn on H-N 16 leads to Lakeshore Road which goes along the lake. Lakeshore Drive or Road, as it is variably called, will hug the Erie shore the majority of the time for the next 30 miles or so.

The road leads to the hamlet of Booth's Harbor. The way to the marina plunges down the face of the high bluff on which the village perches. Here is a large, private marina and waterside diner, the diner providing the only apparent area accessible to the public.

Going east, the peninsula of Turkey Point pulls the shore away from the road for a time. CR 10 returns there at the village of Turkey Point, a sizable cottage and home community with motels and restaurants spread out along the level of the lake. It is quiet here on a chilly but bright Indian Summer forenoon. A few elderly couples stroll arm-in-arm while an onshore wind sends low whitecaps from Long Point Bay skidding to the long beach of Turkey Point Provincial Park. Thousands of wild turkeys roam this area. Once hunted out of existence, they were reintroduced here in the mid-1980's.

Where the shore road ends at a small turnaround at the east end of the village, an elderly woman tends to some flowers growing between the stones of a breakwall across from her cottage.

"We've been at Turkey Point for over 60 years," she explains as she brushes back her white hair. "Although it hasn't been the same since I lost my husband two years ago" she added, a slight catch in her voice. "It's so quiet here. I love it. I call it 'my little bit of heaven.'"

"We only have two busy months in the summer when the kids are out of school. On Sundays it can be a little maddening. I don't even go up there," she said pointing toward the village. "But then fall comes and everybody's gone. It's so peaceful."

Back on Lakeshore Drive, a marker at the provincial park golf course gives a peek at the past. The British began building a fort here in 1813 the following the loss of Fort Amherstburg. After the construction of a blockhouse and part of a palisade the British gave up, its remote location proving to be too much of a challenge.

Turkey Point Provincial Park has 200 sites in two wooded campgrounds, some with electrical hookups, with showers/flush toilets. A hiking trail on a high bluff gives a panoramic view of Lake Erie and the shallow waters of the bay with its extensive beach are ideal for family swimming. For more information, call the park at 519-426-3239.

Continuing east, a narrow river cleaves down toward the lake at Normandale and the Normandale Public Access where a marker tells of the Normandale Furnace built here in 1818. As many as 200 men once toiled here forging iron tools until 1850 when the local supply of bog ore was exhausted. The crystal clear stream that carved this shaded and narrow valley gurgles as it winds around the marker on its rush to the lake. On the road above is the former Union Hotel, a classic two-story nineteenth century inn, now a bed and breakfast. From Normandale, the road climbs a hill away from the lake, winds past the Normandale Cemetery, and to an intersection and right. The road continues and descends to a valley through the hamlet of Fishers Glen and up the hill on the other side to another intersection and another right. Ahead on the right is the Norfolk Conservation Area, a lakeside campground that accommodates year-round trailers and overnight campers. At the entrance to the area a marker tells of a local resident named William Pope, born in 1811, whose paintings, diaries, and journals provided a detailed record of the wilderness that once covered this region. His watercolor paintings of birds are comparable to those of John James Audubon.

The road continues to another valley and Port Ryerse where hillside homes cling to the valley walls. Other than a general store, there's no apparent public access here.

The road heads east from Port Ryerse and splits and Port Ryerse Road goes to the right. About a mile down Port Ryerse Road is the Hay Creek Conservation Area. Here is a campground, picnic ground, and grassy beach shaded by the soft, green needles of a mature white pine forest, a woods majestic in places. The dammed waters of Hay Creek provide the swimming along with a floating dock for diving. Port Ryerse Road ends at Radical Road just beyond the conservation area. Here a right turn leads toward Port Dover. The road becomes Nelson Street West as in enters Port Dover and to Main Street, a.k.a. Ontario 6. Port Dover is actually part of the regional city of Nanticoke which can be confusing.

Main Street slopes toward Lake Erie past an historic town hall and its lofty clock tower, long a landmark for boaters. Huge weights dangle inside and the clock is said to keep perfect time, its 1857 bell tolling on the hour and on the half. Main Street runs down a hill to the harbor district and where the Lynn River meets the lake is a long pier, lighthouse, swimming beach, and retail area with shops, waterside restaurants and pubs. There are also several takeout stands where perch and chips, whitefish and chips, and pickerel and chips are the *entrees du jour.* On soft summer nights this area fills with strollers in an atmosphere that is described as magical.

Over the lift bridge on Ontario 6 and up a hill, John Street descends back to the lake toward a large marina and public park. Port Dover claims to be home to the second largest fresh-water fishery in the world and its commercial fishing fleet is docked on this side of the river. A dozen or so of the squat and muscular boats rock at their docks.

A couple of blocks down 6 from John Street on Don Jon Blvd., a marker tells of the wintering site of the French exploring party of the missionaries Dollier and Galinee. They were the first Europeans to explore the Great Lakes all the way to Sault Ste. Marie and built a residence, chapel, and fort to spend the winter of 1669-70. A wrought iron fence surrounds two mounds of earth, all that remains from that winter spent here over 300 years ago.

Was it a long-suffering winter spent in a remote and wild place far from civilization? On the contrary it was a winter of plenty according to an account written by Gallinee. He extolled of the richness of the land; the plentiful game animals, the abundance of fruits and nuts for gathering, and the wild grapes "as large and as sweet as the finest in France" with which they made wine and with which Dollier said Mass.

He went on to write, "there is assuredly no more beautiful region in Canada," and praised its woods, meadows, and rivers full of fish and beaver. "I leave you to imagine," he teased future historians, "whether we suffered in the midst of this abundance in the earthly Paradise of Canada."

Port Dover features the Harbour Museum, Lighthouse Festival Theatre, summer festivals, and marina facilities within walking distance of downtown. For more information, call the Haldimand-Norfolk Tourist Information Network at 800-699-9038.

From John St., Pansy Avenue which becomes New Lakeshore Drive leads out of town and veers way from the lake for awhile. A spreading brown haze in an otherwise azure blue sky ahead tells of a looming industrial area. The sprawling Stelco steel works soon appears surrounded by miles of barbed wire fence with smoke belching to the sky. Alcohol and cameras are prohibited, a sign at the gate warns.

Riverside Drive wraps around the complex to Rainham Road and right toward the village of Nanticoke. At the edge of town is a 1910 schoolhouse, bell still hanging in the belfry, now the Nanticoke Community Hall. The industrialization of the lake continues here with another large complex, the Nanticoke Generating Station, hard on Lake Erie.

Lakeshore Road resumes its waterside crawl beyond the power plant to Sandusk Road and Peacock Point, a cottage area on a bluff above the lake. The Haldimand Conservation Area here provides camp and day-use facilities on a bluff over the lake.

Out of Peacock Point, Lakeshore Drive leads to Cheapside Road and north to CR 3. Here is a tourist information center and the Wilson MacDonald Memorial School and Museum inside an 1872 schoolhouse. Wilson MacDonald was a poet of renown and a marker in the parking lot highlights his life story.

From the Wilson MacDonald Memorial CR 3 travels east and, after a mile, Wheeler Road travels back toward the lake and to Selkirk Provincial Park, a camping and day use ground with a marsh boardwalk and trails that wind through an oak forest.

Selkirk Provincial Park has 142 campsites in an open setting, some with electrical hookups, and showers/flush toilets. For more information, call the park at 519-426-7650.

Lakeshore Drive resumes briefly along the lake before going inland to a bridge fording a rocky creek. It then joins the lake again to teeter on its bank, curving above water blue against the low October sun on its southern sojourn toward the equator. Land can be seen through the haze on the far shore as the lake is narrowing now and drawing the Canadian and American sides together.

The lake drive continues along a shore solid with cottages with an occasional farm mixed in. Other than a rare variety store, there are no retail businesses or gas stations along here. "It happens in the best of families," an elderly cottage owner chuckles as he hands an inattentive author who let his tank run dry a gasoline can. "Use it all, just be sure to bring the can back."

Later he talks about living on the lake. "It's not just beautiful days like today," he says as he gestures toward the lake and towards golden corn fields across the road framed by scarlet maples and the blue northern sky. "I like being on the water. Even in bad weather, the lake is the last thing I look at before I go to bed and the first thing I look at when I get up. It's like an old friend."

"Sure the winters get a little long but winter can get long no matter where you are," he adds. "Some folks around here go to Florida in the winter but when they get back they talk about how bored they got. I just as soon spend mine here instead of squeezed into some little trailer somewhere." The journey continues and after a time Aikens Road goes north to Kings Row Road to Johnson Road which returns to the shore.

The road continues and an occasional resident fetching the mail or taking a stroll is all that can be seen. Few other vehicles are on the road this day as a dog slumbering along the berm enjoying the warmth of the sun gives a sleepy glance to the passerby interrupting his nap.

The gray stone of Christ Church sits on a curve in the road, an Anglican house of worship built in 1927. Port Maitland Cemetery surrounds the church and reaches to the lake's blue edge.

Just beyond the church is the Grand River and the hamlet of Port Maitland where Esplanade Park guards the mouth of the river as it empties into Lake Erie.

A long fishing pier zigzags out to a harbor light. A man from Cayuga fishes near the end of the pier as he has been for 42 years. "I get the bass in the spring, I get the occasional perch and the pickerel," he says in a clipped, French accent. "In the fall I get the salmon and the rainbow. The pink salmon I don't see this year."

"I used to dip buckets in spring and come up full of smelt," he continues. "Now the (Port) Dover boats take them all. Not a one did I see this spring. You know there used to be 54 of them, the Dover tugs. I don't know how many there are now."

"It's fun," he says of fishing. "I used to bring my kids down and fish with them. Now they're grown and I still come."

The British started a naval base here in 1815 intended to house frigates and 1,000 men. A storm swept away part of the post in 1827 and the rest of the fort was abandoned in 1834. Port Maitland was established in 1820, built its first church in 1846, and in 1850 the town buried 40 bodies, souls lost when the ship Commerce sank offshore. R. R. 11 follows the Grand River north from Port Maitland to H-N 3 and a bridge crossing over to the river city of Dunnville. A riverside town park just north of downtown on Main Street gives the opportunity to view the appropriately named Grand River, its broad, calm expanse stretching hundreds of feet to tall marsh grasses on the far side. A marker at the park looks back at the town's past. In 1829 a feeder canal that connected Lakes Erie and Ontario was opened here and the community thrived as a major shipping center. However by 1845 the second Welland canal was finished and the great ships no longer sailed through Dunnville.

Also on display is an anchor typical of those used by ships in the latter part of the 1800's and found on Lake Erie's bottom in 1985. The wooden stock of the iron anchor is in remarkably good condition. Was it merely lost? Or was it from a boat driven below the waves like so many were in the days before modern shipping? No one knows.

From Dunnville, another Canadian town with a humming downtown area and fine brick homes, H-N 3 leaves via Main Street East and back toward the lake, not to be confused with Ontario 3 which also passes through town, and to Rock Point Provincial Park. Rock Point juts out into the lake here and on this mild afternoon several anglers are casting into the lake's blue waters from the flat rock surface of the point's tip.

The park also has a swimming beach and a boardwalk leading to a viewing platform on a 25-foot high sand dune, sand swept by the wind over the years from the mouth of the Grand River. And hiking trails wind under the canopy of a Carolinian forest, ground that is being carpeted by colorful leaves floating to the earth in a gentle breeze.

As slowly earthward leaf by red leaf slips,
The sad trees rustle on chill misery,
A soft strange inner sound of pain-crazed lips,
That move and murmur incoherently;
As if all leaves, that yet have breath, were sighing
With pale hushed throats, for death is at the door,
So many low soft masses for the dying
Sweet leaves that live no more.

Archibald Lampman, *In October*

Rock Point Provincial Park has 135 campsites, some with electrical hook-ups, and showers/flush toilets. The park also features limestone outcrops that contain fossils dating back 350 million years. For more information, call the park at 905-774-6642.

From Rock Point H-N 3 leads to the village of Lowbanks. Boulders and barriers piled in front of the lakeside cottages are testimony to the source of the village's name. One building that definitely preceded these cottages is the historic looking, white frame building housing the village post office. When was it built? "Can't say with absolute certainty, the postmaster inside informs, "but the year 1821 is written on a beam in the attic so that's when we believe it was built."

Outside Lowbanks, the road name changes to Niagara Region 30 and comes to the Long Beach Conservation Area, a camping and swimming park, closed for the season. Hundreds of picnic tables are stored upright in lines leaning one against the other as if ready to snake dance.

Through the hamlets of Long Beach and Burnaby on N-R 30 stand more clutches of cottages. There are so many cottages on this north shore it would seem that everyone in the province must have one, or know someone who does.

After Burnaby, the road jogs north to Ontario 3 and east to Port Colborne. Here the Welland Canal knifes the city in two as it mediates the 300-foot difference between Lakes Erie and Ontario. Freighters quietly slip through the city and lock number eight, one of the longest on earth, day and night. The world's major languages bounce off these lock walls as it shepherds ships through from both the far side of the lake and the far side of the world.

At the juncture of Ontario 3 and the canal is a tourist information center where a huge lake freighter is squeezing into lock number eight this day. Its great hull appears followed by the long, flat deck that covers the ship's deep cargo holds. Then the superstructure of the stern containing the pilot house and ship's living quarters slides under the lift bridge and into the lock, massive and towering high above the level of the street. Deckhands keep a close watch on the inches that separate the sides of the great ship from canal walls, walls scarred and scraped numerous times over the years. Only the soft and muffled rumble of the ship's engine is heard, making far less noise than a passing truck or bus, vehicles fractional in size and weight.

Just south of the tourist booth is the Lock 8 Fountain View, a terraced rock garden with flowers and a flowing fountain that provides a perch where the entire lock can be viewed.

In Port Colborne's downtown, historic West Street borders the canal, its nineteenth century buildings house shops and restaurants, buildings little changed from the days when the masts of schooners and clipper ships glided by.

One of those schooners, the *USS Stephen Girard,* was treated rather unkindly by the local militia while passing through Port Colborne in 1839. Relations were still a little tense between the United States and Canada from the so-called Patriots Rebellion of 1837-38.

The rebellion was a short-lived and somewhat confused event consisting of skirmishes between Canadian revolutionaries, backed by volunteers and munitions from the United States, against the vastly superior British/Canadian government.

The militia soldiers demanded the flag of the ship and attempted to prevent it from leaving the lock. The captain and crew were barely able to maneuver the ship out of the lock and set sail under a barrage of stones while the stars and stripes was torn to shreds by a jeering mob. When Canadian authorities learned of the incident they sent a letter of apology and a new flag and ordered the arrest and investigation of the of-

Lowbanks, Ontario

Welland Canal-Port Colborne, Ontario

fending soldiers.

Where the Welland Canal meets Lake Erie, Lakeview Park sits high on a bluff and overlooks Sugarloaf Harbor and Gravelly Bay. A strong southerly breeze sweeps off the lake this day dancing in the branches and yellow leaves of aged willow trees here.

The Historical and Marine Museum at King and Princess streets, a collection of buildings in a village setting with over 10,000 artifacts, finds its home in downtown Port Colborne. The museum's yard displays a slab from a tulip tree that broke the earth in 1750 when only Indians and French explorers roamed the area. Its over 200 years of growth rings were witness to the town's evolution from waterside outpost to modern city.

Also in the yard are an anchor from the steamship Raleigh, battered to Lake Erie's bottom when it lost its rudder during a furious 1911 storm, and a hand-operated winch from the days when men muscled the great gates of the canal locks into place.

Port Colborne also has festival theater, a farmer's market, and the modern Sugarloaf Harbor Marina with over 500 slips. For more information, call the Port Colborne Economic Development Office at 888-835-PORT or 905-835-3361.

Leaving Port Colborne, Clarence Street crosses the canal over a lift bridge, its massive steel girder superstructures anchored to each shore. On the east side of the canal is Welland Street. Southbound Welland ends at the kilometer-long Nickel Beach, a public beach. Northbound Welland leads to Ontario 3 east to Sherkston Road which travels south toward the lake where it intersects with Michener Road and east.

A right turn on Ridgeway Road a right leads over a hill and the road ends at the shore and Crystal Beach, the last public beach accessible by road on this north shore. Here a bump of land called Abino Point creates a small bay and beach. The wind this day is kicking up whitecaps on the bay waters and sending currents of sand snaking across the blacktop of the beach road.

It was near here that the captain of a steamer bound for

Buffalo rowed ashore in 1860 to drop off two fleeing slaves he had given passage to. The captain had given little thought toward his passengers until he reached the shore, as he later recalled.

"They said, 'Is this Canada?' I said 'Yes, there are no slaves in this country'; then I witnessed a scene I shall never forget. They seemed to be transformed; a new light shone in their eyes, their tongues were loosed, they laughed and cried, prayed and sang praises, and fell upon the ground and kissed it, hugged and kissed each other crying 'Bless the Lord! Oh! I'm free before I die.' "

From the beach area a one-way road called Terrace Lane leads away from the beach area to Crystal Beach Road to Ridge Road South and north to Thunder Bay Road which goes east along the lake. Thunder Bay Road ends at Stone Mill Road which jogs to Dominion Road.

After several miles on Dominion Road, Bardol Avenue heads back to the lake and to Lakeshore Road and left. Here the tall skyline of the city of Buffalo literally leaps into view across the lake on the New York shore. Here too is the sweeping green lawns of the reconstructed Fort Erie as this Northern Lake Erie shore crawl ends as it began, in a city with a War of 1812 fort. Fort Erie's roots date back almost 250 years. Weary French fur traders, arms heavy with fatigue, dragged their pelt-laden canoes ashore here to trade at a post on the Niagara River. Today it is home to the fort of the same name where was played out a stalemate so characteristic of the War of 1812.

This solid stone fort with high walls and deep trenches has its origins in a wooden fort built by the British in 1764 and eventually laid flat by ice driven ashore in winter storms. Rebuilding began in 1805 and the final chapter of the bloody summer of 1814 was written here as British and Americans battled for control of the Niagara frontier. Thomas Jefferson's confidence at war's beginning that the acquisition of Canada "will be a mere matter of marching" would again prove to be mortally wrong.

On a mid-August dawn the British attacked Fort Erie which they had lost to the Americans earlier in the war. Savage hand-to-hand combat at the parapets ended when a magazine in the north bastion of the fort erupted in a towering sheet of flame, hurling debris and bodies, mostly British, into the air.

The remaining British fled in terror, some falling into the Niagara River where they were swept away. The smell of burning flesh hovered over the ground outside the fort which was left a human wasteland of the dead and the agony of the dying. One officer who reached safety hurled his sword to the ground and sobbed "This is a disgraceful day for Old England." More skirmishes took place in the ensuing weeks before the demoralized British withdrew in September. The following month the Americans, also weakened and dispirited, burned what was left of the fort and crossed the river back to the United States. Thousands of casualties had been suffered over a fort that ultimately neither side wanted.

A monument near the fort marks the spot where the remains of 150 British soldiers who died that August day are buried. During the restoration of the fort in 1938-39 the remains of three American soldiers were discovered and buried here, sleeping forever in peace with their former enemies after sharing final days of blood, bombs, and fear.

Peace Bridge looms in the distance, its steel span links the United States and Canada together, its name speaks to the accord enjoyed between the two countries since the end of the War of 1812. Underneath, the waters of Lake Erie squeeze into the Niagara River where they will eventually thunder over the edge of one of the great waterfalls in the world.

From the fort, Niagara Parkway promenades along the shore. Near Peace Bridge is an elaborate gate and memorial grounds commemorating Canada's war dead and celebrating the friendship between Canada and the United States.

The parkway continues through a small Chinatown to a hill and what may be one of the oldest churches on this north shore, St. Pauls Anglican Church established in 1821. The gray stone and steeple of the church are warmed by an October morning sun rising over the churning waters of the Niagara River. A burying ground slopes away from the church and between the church's twin entrances is a tablet. The stone lists the names of 19 who sleep not here but in Flanders Field, France, killed in the war that was supposed to end all wars.

From the church, Niagara Parkway ducks under the International Railroad Bridge, built in 1873, and to Jarvis Street, Fort Erie's downtown shopping district. Just north of the downtown area on the parkway begins The Niagara River Recreation Trail, 35 miles of paved trail that follows the river from Fort Erie to Niagara-on-the-Lake on Lake Ontario.

The roiling waters of the Niagara River have seen their share of boat traffic over the years but probably none as bizarre as the schooner *Michigan* in September, 1827. Condemned as unseaworthy, she had been bought by Buffalo speculators and sideshow operators seeking to drum up business who circulated handbills telling of their intent to send her down the river and over Niagara Falls.

In a grotesque parody of Noah's Ark the ship was loaded with domestic and wild animals and sent over the falls where it was smashed to splinters on the rocks below. Thousands watched from both sides of the river and falls in a carnival atmosphere in this dubious moment in American and Canadian history.

Fort Erie boasts of year-round festivals and things to do including thoroughbred horse racing, historical, railroad, and antique fire equipment museums, a doll house gallery, Fort Erie tours and military reenactments, tribal pow-wows, a winterfest, and is only 20 miles from Niagara Falls. For more information, call the Fort Erie Economic Development Corp. at 905-871-3232 or the Tourism Hotline at 905-871-8525.

Chapter IV

BUFFALO TO ASHTABULA

From Fort Erie, Peace Bridge arcs over the Niagara River. It's waters, caught in the gravitational pull caused by Niagara Falls which is twenty miles downstream, swirl around the abutments. The bridge descends to the New York shore and Buffalo.

This city, known in more recent years for its chicken wings and Super Bowl frustrations, was once one of the United States' major industrial centers, its largest inland port, and one of the largest producers of steel in the world. As the 1800's drew to a close Buffalo called itself "one of the most rapidly growing cities in the universe." And the *New York Times* agreed that it would "become the greatest milling city on earth" and one that would rival Chicago to claim the title of the Great Lakes' greatest city. Buffalo was a city of stately office buildings, of millionaire's mansions, and a destination for tourists from the then frumpy town of Toronto to sample its dining, shopping, culture, and entertainment.

But by the 1970's the "Rust Belt" syndrome of industrial and civic decline that staggered many Midwest and Eastern American cities had hit Buffalo particularly hard and shuttered factories, a dying downtown, and a dwindling population base marked the "Queen City of the Lakes" as a city in trouble.

On January 26, 1977 Buffalo, already in the grip of record-cold winter that had seen snow fall since October and locked

Lake Erie in a three foot layer of ice, saw a blizzard of epic power roar in from the west. Tens of thousands were stranded in downtown buildings while thousands more shivered in snowbound cars throughout the area. Downtown Buffalo became a black and white ghost town.

The wind howled for days, great snow clouds blew in off the lake, and fires burned out of control as roads were blocked by enormous drifts. The storm brought out humanity's best and worst as countless Buffalo residents performed heroic acts of rescue and assistance while others looted businesses.

When the storm abated a massive and expensive cleanup started as the snow, with no more place to plow it, had to be dug out with huge front-end loaders and hauled from the downtown area. It was dumped in the Niagara River, loaded into empty train cars headed south, and piled into dirty mountains in the city parks. Spring finally came and in late April came a vivid reminder of how bad things had been when the melting snows of one of the city park snow mountains revealed a four-door Pontiac sedan.

As the winter of 1977 faded into memory Buffalonians, galvanized in part by their shared experience of fighting the blizzard, rolled up their collective sleeves and began to dig away at the city's decline and the late 1970's and 1980's saw a slow renaissance. Now its downtown is a mix of modern buildings that rose from the shadows of its decaying years and of the architectural splendor of historic buildings built during Buffalo's boom years in the late 19th and early 20th centuries.

From the bridge, a brief jog on I-190 leads to Exit 8 and Niagara Street and south to the hub of downtown Buffalo, Niagara Square. Here the massive art deco edifice of Buffalo City Hall dominates the scene. The broad sandstone building, finished in 1931, exudes majesty and authority. Colorful tiles and carved friezes of scenes from Buffalo's past grace its exterior.

At the center of the square is a large fountain and 62-foot white marble obelisk dedicated to President William McKinley who was assassinated in Buffalo in 1901. McKinley was "victim of a treacherous assassin who shot the president as he was extending to him the hand of courtesy" an inscription on the monument notes. Buffalo felt the shame then that Dallas felt in 1963 when President John F. Kennedy was killed in that city. Niagara Street continues through the square to Pearl Street. A block to the right at the intersection of Church Street is the Guaranty Building whose all steel frame made it one of the world's first skyscrapers in 1895. The graceful Louis Sullivan-designed structure almost fell to the wrecking ball in the early 1980's but the forces of preservation stood in the way and the Guaranty's terra cotta exterior and art and glasswork of its lobby and interior were restored. It is an internationally recognized work of architecture today. Church Street ends at Main Street which is now a long pedestrian mall with a variety of shops, restaurants, and a shopping mall. Vehicles no longer travel this section of Main Street but, for the footweary shopper, the Metro Rail does. Along the blocks of Main Street can be found more historic buildings, including the Buffalo Savings Bank at Main and Huron Streets, a granite beauty built in 1901 and topped with a glittering gold leaf dome.

In the 600 block of Main Street is a Theater District, home to six theaters and the Market Arcade, an Italian Renaissance Revival structure built in 1892 and patterned after the famed Burlington Arcade in London. Inside the arcade is the Buffalo Visitor Center with information and maps including a downtown walking tour of historic sites.

Throughout the downtown area street names like Seneca, Genessee, and Mohawk give this city a distinctive New York state feel just as King, Queen, and Princess streets common to the towns on the Canadian shore reflect that country's British roots.

Pearl Street leads from the downtown area and ends at the Buffalo River and Naval and Servicemen's Park, the largest inland naval park in the country. Here ships of war including the cruiser *U.S.S. Little Rock,* with its massive, gray superstructure, are permanently docked and open for tours.

Down the river toward Lake Erie is more parkland, waterside walkways, and the Erie Basin Marina, undoubtedly the only marina anywhere designed in the shape of a bison. An observation tower at the end of the marina drive (Erie Blvd.) gives a nice view of the lake and Buffalo's renovated waterfront.

It was from Buffalo that the first steamship to sail Lake Erie was launched in 1818. The *Walk-in-the-Water,* named for a Wyandot chief, both amazed and frightened residents of the south shore of Lake Erie on her maiden cruise. For here was a ship with no oars slicing rapidly through the waves in a light wind with a pipe belching dark smoke. For some, this was clearly the work of the devil!

The *Walk-in-the Water* sailed Lakes Erie, Huron, and Michigan for three summers to rave reviews. But she left Buffalo on the afternoon of October 31, 1821 and was battered by an all night gale. By morning she had been beached near the foot of Main Street where all the passengers were rescued, terrified but alive. The ship was damaged beyond repair.

From the downtown area New York 5, also known as the Skyway, arches high along the Lake Erie shore providing a spectacular exit from the city. From this vantage Lake Erie's waters shimmer under a low October sun as the Canadian shore fades from view. On the inward side of the Skyway a literal forest of grain elevators, hundreds of them, sprouts from an industrial landscape. Many of the hulking and aging elevators are abandoned, silent witnesses to Buffalo's once booming economic past.

The Skyway descends to terra firma-what an interesting drive that must be when the snow flies-and New York 5 rolls through the town of Lackawanna whose name used to be synonymous with steel. The great open hearth furnaces of Bethlehem Steel that once produced millions of tons of steel and provided tens of thousands of jobs here have gone forever dark.

In addition to the above snapshot, Buffalo features the Theodore Roosevelt National Inaugural Historic Site, Our Lady of Victory National Shrine, an art museum, science museum, a number of specialized galleries, museums, and art centers, zoological gardens, historical society, and botanical gardens. In addition it is home to Triple A baseball played in a state-of-the-art downtown stadium, N.H.L. hockey in a brand-new downtown arena, and N.F.L. football in suburban Orchard Park. Cruise ships depart downtown Buffalo to ply Lake Erie and the Niagara River and downtown is only minutes away from Niagara Falls. For more information call The Buffalo Visitor Center at 1-800-Buffalo.

New York 5 continues curving west as it traces the Lake Erie shore. Just west of Mount Vernon in Wanakah, Old Lakeshore Drive splits off of New York 5 and travels along the lake, a road also called the Seaway Trail. Old mansions and walled estates face the lake on this drive, some baronial and wrought-iron-gated. Their trees are alive with color and dropping leaves gently to the ground. Just beyond a replica lighthouse on the right that marks the entrance to the Sturgeon Point Water Treatment Plant, Sturgeon Point Road leads back to the lake where the Town of Evans has a large, public marina and fishing pier. Early settlers once dragged in the giant fish here for which this rocky point was named. To the east, the Buffalo skyline is barely visible now.

Wendt Beach, a county park once a private estate, lies beyond Sturgeon Point. A white manor house graces a bluff on the lake, its old bay windows reflecting the waves pounding on the swimming beach below, sand littered with smooth, black shale. The former stables and carriage house of the estate remain, recalling the days when horses romped in pastures now converted to picnic grounds and soccer fields.

The Seaway Trail passes through Evans Town Park, a sizable park that straddles the road. On the left is a large picnic area with a tunnel under the road that leads to more picnic areas and a beach on the right. A smaller lakeside park lies ahead in the town of Lake Erie Beach, a newer park with plans for further expansion.

Evangola State Park lies beyond Lake Erie Beach, a sprawling area with substantial picnic grounds that slope to a low bluff over the lake. With hundreds of tables spread over grassy and shaded ground, it doesn't seem possible that one could come here and not get a table. On this mild Indian Summer day, only one table is taken as V formations of Canada geese sail overhead.

Evangola State Park has 83 campsites in a mostly open setting, some with electrical hookups, and showers/flush toilets. For more information, call the park at 716-549-1760.

The Seaway Trail rejoins New York 5 and continues to the

town of Silver Creek where the creek of the same name has carved a winding path through town. Here is a pretty town square faced by the white spire of First United Presbyterian Church, founded in 1812, and by a 1921 theater, preserved and still a place of entertainment.

The steamboat *Erie* was sailing offshore from Silver Creek on a warm August night in 1841. Bound for Chicago and loaded with immigrants and all their worldly possessions and dreams, she had just received a fresh coat of paint in Buffalo.

But the painters had left some open cans of turpentine which caught fire and turned the ship into a floating inferno. Screaming passengers hurled themselves into the water. Other ships raced to the scene but for approximately 175 souls it was too late, their American Dream coming to an end on Lake Erie's sandy bottom.

Also on the bottom were the life savings of the immigrants, in gold and silver, that had been meant to buy land and homes in middle America. Salvagers who raised the remains of the ship years later were said to have profited from their enterprise.

New York 5 rolls out of Silver Creek and on to the city of Dunkirk. Here a right turn on Serval Street leads to Lakefront Boulevard which curves along the shore. Couples walk hand-in-hand as an old man casts his fishing rod, perhaps hoping to catch his supper.

Lakefront Boulevard rejoins New York 5 briefly which rolls to the long Dunkirk city pier. More fishermen try their luck here as a couple of commercial fishing boats gently rock at their docks, battered and rusty. To the west the giant Niagara Mohawk power plant dominates the scene, its tremendous piles of coal waiting to power the plant's giant turbines.

In the summer of 1812 a salt boat being pursued by a British cruiser took refuge here. The cruiser anchored offshore and lowered a boat with 13 men to capture its prey. Unknown to the British sailors a small militia had been stationed here for just such an occasion and opened fire. Only three of the British escaped being killed or wounded.

Dunkirk's main street, Central Avenue, goes south from the pier and at Sixth Street is the Adams Art Gallery housed in an ornate former Unitarian Church built in 1907. Across the street is the Dunkirk Free Library, a Carnegie Library, built during the same era.

Beyond the city pier on New York 5, Point Drive East leads to the well-preserved grounds of the 1876 Dunkirk Lighthouse and keeper's cottage, now a museum. Point Drive West wraps around to the large picnic grounds of Point Gratiot Park on a bluff over the lake.

The Adams Art Gallery and gift shop is open afternoons Wednesday through Sunday. Admission is free. The stone tower of the Dunkirk Historical Lighthouse and ten-room museum in the brick keeper's cottage are open for tours from April through November. For more information, call 716-366-5050.

New York 5 rolls west out of Dunkirk to Lake Erie State Park, yet another large lakeside park with camping, swimming, and spreading lawns for picnicking.

Lake Erie State Park 97 campsites, none with electrical hookups, and showers/flush toilets. For more information, call the park at 716-792-9214.

The Pennsylvania state line draws nearer as New York 5 continues west and the air fills with the sweet smell of grapes wafting from roadside vineyards. Their vines queue up and down the low hills and hang heavy with the violet fruit. The lake provides a steadying hand to the moods of Mother Nature along the shore as winter-chilled water prevents a too early spring budding and summer-warmed water keeps the first frost at arm's length late into the fall.

This year a too dry summer and a very wet and cloudy September have delayed ripening. This day the grapes eagerly drink in a warm October sun so critical to achieving proper sugar levels and a successful crop.

The vineyards are interrupted by the town of Barcelona where the V of a breakwall stabs into the lake creating a harbor guarded by an old stone lighthouse on the bluff above. The lighthouse is on private property but a plate bolted above its door and viewed with binoculars says it was built by the federal government in 1829 which would make it one of the older lighthouses on the Great Lakes.

There's a small park with a tourist information booth near the lighthouse with a sign that tells the story of the Seaway Trail which travels 450 miles from Ripley to Massena, New York along Lakes Erie and Ontario and the Niagara and St. Lawrence Rivers.

Beyond Barcelona, New York 5 crosses the state line and becomes Pennsylvania 5. The road continues through grape country and comes to the Mazza Vineyards Winery. Inside, vintages are being sampled including one recalling some Lake Erie history, Commemorative Red, its label telling of the Battle of Lake Erie.

From the winery, the road plunges downhill to Pennsylvania 89 which jogs to the north ends at the lake shore and the sands of Freeport Beach. Here is a small park named for Halli Reid, the first woman to swim across Lake Erie. A plaque on a boulder tells that she left Long Point, Ontario the evening of August 8, 1993 and swam all night, arriving here at 10 a.m. the next day. Her picture is also on the rock, that of the smiling young woman walking from the surf at Freeport Beach after what must have been an exhausting but triumphant night.

About a mile inland on Pennsylvania 89 (Lake St.) is the Borough of North East, a bit of serendipity. At the northern edge of town is a branch campus of Mercyhurst College, opened in 1991, on the hilly grounds of an old seminary. On the over 80-acre campus are stone buildings that date back more than 100 years including a Gothic chapel and a small, stone observatory that pokes out of a vineyard. Entering the downtown area, Gibson Park occupies a square sheltered by lanky, old maple trees in autumn blaze this day. In the center of the park is an 1890 fountain with a statue of a goddess, the spray of its water shimmering in the midday sun. Victorian homes and old churches line the streets facing the park. And the brick and stone buildings of the historic downtown shopping district, where you can park for a penny at a flowerpot-topped meter, are in excellent repair.

If the smell of grapes from the vineyards that surround the town doesn't remind you that this is grape country, the large Welch's processing at plant the south edge of town will. And the nickname of the North East's public schools sports teams? The Grapepickers.

Back on Pennsylvania 5 and west is the Penn Shore Winery inside of which is a bit of Pennsylvania wine history. There were several wineries in the North East area until Prohibition dried them up in 1918. None reopened after Prohibition and the area remained wineless until 1968 when the state passed legislation allowing wineries to produce and sell wine on their premises.

Pennsylvania 5 continues and travels to the city of Erie where the road becomes East Lake Road, a.k.a. Alternate 5. At a point where the road narrows from four lanes back to two is Lighthouse Drive, which leads to an 1867 lighthouse. While the sandstone tower appears to be on private property it can be easily viewed from a small public park adjacent to it.

East Lake Road comes to East Drive which heads north toward Lake Erie and Bayfront Highway. Bayfront Highway travels to Erie's bustling and burgeoning harbor, a blend of the old and the new. The golden onion domes of a Russian Orthodox church glimmer in the sun above the harbor area which has a newly built public library and Maritime Museum complex. Also new to the waterfront is a pier with a 157 foot observation tower opened in 1995 to commemorate Erie's 200th birthday. The tower shadows the brig *Niagara,* Commodore Oliver Hazard Perry's flagship in the Battle of Lake Erie. It was here that Perry built his fleet and sailed in 1813 defeating the British fleet from Amherstburg. Scuttled the following year, the *Niagara* was rebuilt after its remains were pulled from the mud 100 years later and she now sails from Erie's harbor again.

From the waterfront State Street, downtown Erie's main artery, climbs to the business district. It passes the Greek Revival facade of the Erie Art Museum, splits Perry Square in two, and goes by the Warner Theater between 8th and 9th streets.

The Warner Brothers commissioned the building of this elegant 1,500 seat theater in 1931 and its gold and silver-leafed art deco interior is being brought back to its original splendor. Under the marquee this day, workers are polishing the elaborate ticket booth and its walls of copper, brass, and nickel. After a few wipes of their cloths, the dulled metal ignites in the afternoon sun. A block east of the theater is a new baseball stadium where the Class A Erie Sea Wolves play. The team is scheduled to move up to AA ball in 1999.

From Perry Square, West 6th Street leaves downtown past the old buildings of Gannon University and the Erie County Court House and segues into Millionaire's Row, an avenue of historic mansions and churches. Some of the fine old mansions remain private homes while others now house social organizations, law offices, and bed and breakfasts. The elaborate edifice of First Presbyterian Church of the Covenant looks like one that might grace an avenue in Paris or Cologne.

West Sixth Street continues out of Erie proper to Peninsula Drive and right to Presque Isle State Park. This day-use sandy peninsula sweeps miles into the lake and is a virtual recreational archipelago for boating, fishing, swimming, hiking, and birding, to name some, flocked to by over four million people annually.

The power of wind and lake created this sand spit and, like Long Point on the Canadian shore, continue to craft it. French for "almost an island," Presque Isle has actually been an island number of times over the years when Lake Erie storms have slashed its tenuous connection to the mainland.

On this quintessentially perfect Indian Summer day, a soft southern breeze slides under a cathedral ceiling of aspens resplendent in amber blaze along the roadway that snakes the length of the peninsula. Off the main road, an azure blue sky frames the red of maples and yellow of marsh grasses painted on the surface of hushed lagoons. The park hums with walkers, bicyclists, and late season sunbathers. Many sit quietly on benches or picnic tables as if alone in a chapel, their faces tilted slightly toward the sky, knowing how precious and short-lived such autumn days are.

So often when Northerners are asked by those from warmer places what they like about living in the North, they cite "the season's change" as a primary reason. And it is the soul- nourishing embrace of days such as this that flash through their mind when they have such conversations. High pressure off the coast of the Carolinas is creating this autumnal heaven this day. But a deep storm system swirling in the Northern Great Plains laden with icy, Canadian air will soon blow this weather to bits. Within a day a cold, driving rain pouring from a leaden sky will strip leaves from the trees while an angry, gray lake pounds the sandy shore, beauty of a different sort.

Erie also features the well-regarded Erie Playhouse with performances year-round, the Gannon University Historical Museum and Discovery Square, a complex of historical and educational activities. For more information, call the Erie Area Convention and Visitors Bureau at 814-454-7191. Presque Isle State Park also features 13 miles of hiking trails, nearly six miles of paved, multipurpose trail, and miles of guarded and unguarded beaches. For more information, call the park at 814-838-8776.

From Peninsula Drive, West lake Street, a.k.a. Alternate 5 leads away from Presque Isle and joins Pennsylvania 5 as it slants southwest along the lakeshore. A wooded road winds to the shore at Lake City and to Lake Erie Community Park, a camp and day-use area. The shore, which was virtually at foot level at Presque Isle less than 10 miles back now laps nearly 100 feet below against a sheer bluff. Gulls floating on the lake's surface look like scattered bits of paper as the broad blue waters span north until they melt into the haze on the horizon. Beyond Lake City is Elk Creek Access Park where Elk Creek has carved its path through forested hills on its course toward the lake. At the entrance is a picnic area while down a sharp hill is fishing and boat access sheltered by high valley walls.

A couple dozen anglers are taking advantage of the weather and fishing from the bank, in small boats, or by wading in the lazy waters of the stream. "Steelies," says one pulling on his rubber waders of his desired catch of the day, steelhead trout. "It's right around now they begin to move upstream," he explained, adding that steelhead remain upstream through the winter before coming back down in the spring. "They're a great fish," he said. "They put up a hell of a fight."

From Elk Creek Pennsylvania 5 continues west where it ends at US 20 near the Ohio state line. US 20 rolls into the Buckeye State and into Conneaut which is tucked into the extreme northeast corner of Ohio. US 20 goes into Conneaut's downtown and a left on Main Street goes by its 1876 town hall. Just beyond the town hall, Buffalo Street goes to the right past the 1908 Carnegie Library and ends after several blocks at Depot Street and the Conneaut Railroad Museum, housed in the former New York Central Depot.

In the museum yard are several old trains cars led by a hulking, black, steam locomotive once Engine Number 755 of the New York, Chicago, and St. Louis line. The mighty engine's wheels are now frozen near an old, stone mile marker it once thundered past. Ninety-nine miles to Buffalo and 425 miles to Chicago, the marker says.

Going east on Depot Street leads to Broad Street and left to Ohio 531 and the lake. On this road is Conneaut Township Park, a rolling expanse of sandy beach along with lakeside and hilltop picnic areas. The city and township of Conneaut voted in 1926 to create this place and mature trees grace its well-kept grounds. Below and to the east is Conneaut's harbor.

It was from this harbor that the railroad car ferry *Marquette and Bessemer No. 2* steamed out on a stormy December day in 1909 and into eternity. The ship left on its daily five hour crossing to Port Stanley in a rising gale on a Tuesday morning.

She carried 30 rail cars, a crew of 31, and a last second passenger who literally jumped on the ship as it pulled away, a businessman allegedly carrying $50,000. She was a sturdy craft only a few years old and specifically designed to plow such heavy seas.

The storm deepened and nightfall was met by a blinding snow and a plunging thermometer. A customs agent at Port Stanley thought he saw the ship's gray, wallowing, silhouette fighting to make the narrow harbor entrance before giving up and heading west, perhaps for the protection of Erieau.

She was never seen again.

Residents on both shores reported hearing blasts from the ship's whistle during the night, distress calls as the doomed ferry desperately battled mountainous seas searching for safe harbor. Some emerged from their homes with lanterns, only to see a wall of white. By Wednesday morning the storm had abated but there was no ship to be seen and no more distress calls heard.

A frantic search of the lake ensued in hopes that the ship might be found somewhere, wounded but safe. The following Sunday the tug Commodore Perry, sailing 15 miles off of Erie, was about to give up the search when the telescope of Captain Jerry Driscoll spotted a lifeboat, according to an account in *The Toledo Daily Blade.* As the tug rushed toward the scene, Driscoll could see several of the men sitting upright. "By appearance they were alive, but sat very still, with their heads hanging down and their eyes closed. 'They're exhausted,' said Capt. Driscoll." No answers to the calls of the crew were received as the tug drew near and, as its sailors peered into the boat, they shuddered as they discovered the reason why. "The faces were not pale; they seemed to glow with almost unusual health, but the bodies, faces and all, were frozen stiff and solid in death." The boat bobbed on low waves with a grisly cargo of nine silent victims. Lightly clad, they had abandoned ship in a hurry. The clothes of another were frozen in the ice covering the lifeboat's bottom.

"At first there had been 10 in the boat but one had become mad at the horror of it and snatched off his clothes and bared his shivering body to the killing gale and then leaped into the black water," the newspaper article speculated in the prose of the day. A few more victims eventually washed to shore and the body of the first mate was pulled from a Niagara River ice jam the following spring. The last to be surrendered by the lake was that of the captain whose corpse came ashore at Long Point the following October. The rest of those who sailed on the *Marquette and Bessemer No. 2*'s condemned final voyage never were found.

Was there a tenth passenger in the lifeboat driven crazy by fear who stripped and jumped into the lake? What was the doomed ship's desperate course that long last night and how could the pleas for help of its whistle have been heard on both sides of the lake? What caused her to sink in seas she was designed and engineered to withstand? Was the unlucky last second passenger really carrying $50,000? The answers lie beneath the waves.

The lake carefully guards the grave of the *Marquette and Bessemer No. 2* as the efforts of collectors and treasure hunters over time have been for naught. She probably sleeps somewhere off of Long Point in the deepest part of Lake Erie along with the 18 souls that the lake never surrendered. It was an anguished Christmas for many residents of this village in 1909 as the majority of the crew and their families made their homes here.

West from Conneaut on Ohio 531 is North Kingsville Sunset Park, a spot of land above the lake with picnic tables and a walking trail. From here can be seen the orange orb of the sun on its afternoon journey west.

The highway continues through an industrial area to Ashtabula where Lakeshore Park lies. Similar to the park at Conneaut, its broad lawns sweep to the level of the lake. Porch swings hanging from beams in the lakeside shelter house rock gently in the breeze as the afternoon shadows lengthen and couples stroll on the beach. A hillside pond is home to a flock of white geese being fed by a young mother and her child. Geese block the road to see what is going on, in no hurry to move whatsoever.

The road descends into the valley of the Ashtabula River, Indian for "river of many fish," and its historic harbor. Moses Cleaveland passed through here in 1796 on his way to found the city that bears his name and convinced surveyors that the river be named "Mary Esther" for his favorite daughter. The name lasted about as long as did the two gallons of wine he bribed the surveyors with. After a slow start "The Harbor" as it was known then came to be one of the busiest ore and coal docks in the world by the 1870's. Its streets were an ethnic tapestry woven from the various European immigrant groups and of sailors from other lands, their native tongues filling the valley with a medley of languages. With the many sailors came the "color" they bring. There would be as many as 600 mariners in port every day during shipping season. As a result, Ashtabula Harbor came to be known as the roughest port on the Great Lakes with more saloons than any other known port save for Singapore on the other side of the earth.

Although the great fleets of ships are gone, Ashtabula is still a busy port. An historic business district crawls up Bridge Street on the river's west side, its century old buildings built

Ashtabula, Ohio

during the harbor's glory days home to taverns, restaurants, and shops. From Bridge Street, Hulbert Street is a cobblestone climb to Walnut Street and Point Park that gives a sweeping view of Ashtabula's working harbor. Great piles of coal and stone rise from the flats of the restless harbor valley as trains with long chains of hopper cars, almost looking like a model railroad from this distance, move in and out.

A long conveyor belt arcs high over the river bringing coal from the east side of the valley to the west where it is being loaded into a lake freighter while another one awaits. On display in the park is an old, iron machine standing about 12 feet high with two muscular maws and an operator's cab on top.

"That's an old coal loader," an elderly woman sitting on a nearby bench informs. "My brother used to run one but that was a long time ago. It was a rough, dirty job," she added. "We used to badger him about it because we were afraid he'd get hurt or killed someday. He finally took a job in town."

Across from the park is a marine museum and on its north side facing the lake is the pilot house from the ship *Thomas Walters,* moored permanently to a grassy bluff. Inside, the old wooden helm stands, still surrounded by charts, compasses, and all the other workings that once guided the ship through the five Great Lakes.

As the slanting sun begins to leave the valley, a siren wails and the old steel girder lift bridge spanning the Ashtabula River raises skyward to allow a couple of sailboats to pass on their way to some late autumn afternoon sailing. With a forecast of rain and plunging temperatures, such opportunity might not come again this year.

Ashtabula is home to the Great Lakes Marine and U.S. Coast Guard Memorial Museum and the annual Blessing of the Fleet. For more information, call the Ashtabula Chamber of Commerce at 216-998-6998.

Chapter V:

GENEVA-ON-THE-LAKE TO CLEVELAND

After nearly a week of clouds and damp chill the sun returns this morning, warming the colors of the season, hues muted to copper and rust but still pleasantly interrupted by the golden burst of a sugar maple or the maroon majesty of a red oak daubed against the deep blue sky. Shadows slant across the road now as the sun continues its southern sojourn.

> The earth is the cup of the sun,
> That he filleth at morning with wine,
> With the warm, strong wine of his might
> From the vintage of gold and of light
> Fills it, and makes it divine.
>
> Archibald Lampman, *The Sun Cup*

Ohio 531 leaves Ashtabula and continues its travel along the lake and rolls into Geneva-on-the-Lake where the sprout of motels, cottages, taverns, and open-air restaurants lining the road announce a summer resort, one that empties after Labor Day. A number of cottage rentals with lake views are here but virtually no sand lies between the lake and the shore, a beach town with no beach. There's a township park here on the lake, its shelter house on a waterside bluff. Many older and well kept homes share the bluff as well through the town. At the west edge of town is Geneva State Park's Chestnut

Grove Picnic Area, a spacious ground shaded by a symmetrical stand of maple trees planted in rows many years ago. The lake cuts deeply into the bluff at the west end of the grove and rocks have been dumped into the crevice to slow the erosion. The surf washes over a graveyard of trees on the shore below, recent victims to the power of the lake.

From the picnic ground, Ohio 534 jogs south briefly to the entrance to Geneva State Park where a winding, forested road gives access to the park's campground, a fair-sized swimming beach, cabins, and a large, modern marina. Ample privacy awaits cool weather campers this day after a stretch of poor weather, as only a couple of sites are spoken for.

Geneva-on-the-Lake also features the Jennie Munger Gregory Memorial, one of the first frame houses built on Lake Erie's southern shore, and an annual grape festival. For more information, call the Convention and Visitors Bureau at 216-466-8600. Geneva State Park has 91 sites, all with electrical hookups, and showers/flush toilets. For more information, call the park at 216-466-8400.

The road through the park continues to Countyline Road and south to Vrooman Road and then west to Dock Street. Where Dock Street meets the lake lies the Arcola Creek Estuary, one of the few remaining estuaries on the shores of the Great Lakes. The waters of river and lake combine here in a spreading wetland to create a unique environment where steelhead salmon spawn and migratory birds find succor.

A murky brown river emerges from the estuary and slices through the rocky shore and into the lake. Only the gentle trickle of water can be heard this day. There is no reminder of the smoke and the shouts of men that filled the air here in the early to mid 1800's from the thriving foundry of the Arcole Iron Works. The works was at one time the largest industry in Ohio, employing 2,000 men. Its furnaces glowed until 1840 when supply of bog ore harvested from the estuary was exhausted. The town of Ellensburg grew around the foundry, a shipbuilding town where the keel of the first steamship built west of Buffalo was laid. More ships were launched into Lake Erie here during the early 1800's than from any other lake port and ships continued to be built here until 1863. By then the forests of the area had been cleared of trees and no more wood was available and the town was abandoned. Like the iron works, Ellensburg exists now only in the pages of history.

South on Dock Street, Lake Road East jogs west to Bennett Road and south to Lake Road and to Madison-on-the-Lake. The town park wraps around an old ball diamond where the crack of the bat has floated out over the lake on many a summer night. A walkway edges a sycamore-lined bank over a brief beach here, a beach anchored by concrete groins needed to keep the lake at arm's length. A rusty sign on a leaning pole warns swimmers that they do so at their own risk.

From the park, Lake Road leaves town and ends at Redbird Road which goes south to Chapel Road. Chapel Road goes west to a left on McMackin Road which journeys south to US 20 and away from the lake for awhile.

US Routes. It was on these roads that people crossed the country in the days before they zipped over interstate highways. It was a slower but richer way to travel as the unique flavors of the passing villages and cities, states and regions, could be discovered and tasted, an opportunity lost on our efficient but insulated modern highways.

Along US 20 a row of lime green buildings, once vacationer's cottages, are monthly apartments now. The Lake Breeze Motel is still here although vines curl around the neon tubing of its rusty sign. But most of the old motels where route travelers once slept and the diners where they ate are gone now, replaced by ones owned by corporate chains and crowded around interstate exits. As a means of long distance travel, US routes harken to the era of Packards, car hops, and the novelty of black and white television.

The four lanes of US 20 pass through North Perry and its twin nuclear plant cooling towers in the distance and to Ohio 535 which slants back toward the lake through an industrial area and to Fairport Harbor. Here East Street at the edge of town travels to Second Street and to the lake.

Anchored to a rise above the harbor is an historic lighthouse, its weathered sandstone exterior readying to face its 125th winter, its keeper's cottage now a museum. Down a sweep of grass below is Fairport Harbor Lakefront Park, a beach and park with new buildings, walkways, and parking lots.

The Grand River meets the lake here, a river once called the Kichisibi, Indian for "big river." An 1899 description of Fairport Harbor called it a major "port of hail" for ships from Cleveland and other lake ports. The ships still hail here and one of these great freighters glides beyond the protective arms of the harbor's long breakwalls while another patiently waits to enter. The black smoke rising from the waiting ship's stack trails to the north. From the lighthouse, High Street heads south to Ohio 283 and across the Grand River and through the village of the same name. On the west side of the village is Ohio 44, a four lane highway, which goes north and ends at the day-use Headlands Beach State Park.

Entering the park and passing by the tall shaft of the Morton Salt mine near its gate brings back decades-old memories; of childhood Saturdays and trips to this beach in a 1954 powder blue Pontiac sedan; of sun, swimming, and sandwiches in which some grains of sand always found their way; and of heat shimmering over crowds of sunbathers listening to Cleveland Indians games on transistor radios.

There were always a few dead fish back then. Then lots of them. Then great schools of them, their lifeless eyes floating in to shore. And then there were no more trips to the beach. "The lake is too dirty," parents told their children. "We can't go there anymore." And the children couldn't understand why this happened.

But that was a long time ago and the Lake Erie of the 1960's and of the 1990's are almost as different as night and day. The beach at Headlands is once again a place of swimming, sandy sandwiches, and sunbathers listening to an Indians game, now on a boombox.

The fine sand beach here is a sprawling one, almost a mile-long and over 100 yards wide in places, it is the largest natural beach in Ohio. The berms that segregate the large parking areas are lined with thousands of mature cottonwoods. In dormancy for the winter now, their brown leaves swirl and rattle across sandy parking lots.

Here too is the Headlands Dunes State Nature Reserve. The original dunes here, like most around the lake, were leveled in

Madison-On-The-Lake, Ohio

Headlands Dunes State Nature Reserve, Ohio

the name of "progress." But a rebirth began in 1976 when the state reintroduced simple beach grasses which grab and hold sand sent to them by the wind. Now this sculpture of sand grows a little larger every year.

Headlands Drive travels west from the park across a low bridge spanning the northern end of the Mentor Marsh State Nature Preserve, a winding wetland abutting Marsh Creek. At the top of the hill on the far side of the bridge is a parking lot and trailhead. A marker here tells that the marsh was designated a natural history landmark in 1965 because of its value in demonstrating the natural history of the United States.

Headlands Drive ends at Jordan Drive which jogs to Corduroy Road. A few blocks south on Corduroy is Woodbridge Lane on the right. At lane's end is the Carl and Mary Newhous Overlook, a viewing platform that allows an appreciation of the lushness and breadth of Mentor Marsh. A sea of tall marsh grass sighs gently in the wind here as if telling the visitor that this is a place of quiet. Woodbridge Lane leads back to Corduroy Road and south where a causeway crosses the marsh. Grasses rising high above the surface of the road wave vehicles across. Atop a hill on the far side is the Mentor Marsh Visitor Center. From here, Corduroy Road continues to Ohio 283 and west.

Along Ohio 283 the suburban collar of the Cleveland metropolitan area begins to tighten and the town park at Mentor-on-the-Lake where 283 turns left provides refuge. A Depression-era shelter house shaded by a stately oak tree sits on a lakeside butte here over a beach that is rocky and prohibitive. Children play in a valley that divides this pleasant waterside stop as the sun makes its afternoon journey toward the lake.

From Mentor-on-the Lake Ohio 283, also known as Lakeshore Boulevard, rolls along the shore into the city of Eastlake and over the Chagrin River and a marina thick with boats. Beyond the river valley a short distance and on a hill to the left is the Eastlake City Hall and the Boulevard of 500 flags.

Adjacent to and curving around the rear of city hall and into a memorial garden fly 500 American flags. To the staff of each is attached names of area veterans. A stiff breeze makes this unique memorial a kaleidoscope of red, white, and blue, a sight enhanced by the sound of 500 flags snapping in the wind. The sound of the flags drowns out the noise of nearby traffic.

Lake Shore Boulevard continues into Willowick and by the Willowick Municipal Center, where a public park sits on a bluff over the lake, and on into the suburb of Euclid. Here older brick apartment buildings, along with lakeside high rises, become numerous as the road is traveling through Lake Erie's largest and most heavily populated metropolitan area.

In Euclid is Kenneth J. Sims park, a sizable lakefront park with stately trees once the estate of a Cleveland industrialist. The 1923 brick manor house has been preserved and is undergoing renovation and features oak paneling, carved wood, and beveled, leaded glass. Lake Shore Boulevard continues passing by numbered cross streets and to East 185th Street, the eastern limits of the city of Cleveland.

The entrance to the Villa Angela and Wildwood Areas of Cleveland Lakefront State Park soon appears on the right. Cleveland Lakefront State Park (C.L.S.P) consists of six separate areas at various locations on the Cleveland shoreline and is visited by millions every year. Several of the areas were former city parks turned over to the state in the 1970's when Cleveland's economic woes drastically reduced park funding.

A pretty stone bridge painted white crosses over Euclid Creek here to a large marina and park area. Boat ramps, boardwalks, a swimming beach, and fishing piers are some of the amenities the two areas offer. Some urban anglers try their luck in the creek while some old men play chess on this pleasant autumn late afternoon. A short distance down Lake Shore Boulevard is the Euclid Beach Area of C.L.S.P. with its picnic grounds, sizable swimming beach, and with facilities still being added as of this writing.

The road continues and passes by a grand gate once the entrance to Euclid Beach Park. Twin stone towers connected by a sign bearing the former park's name are all that remain of the large amusement park that once spread over many acres here. The park, built in 1895 and patterned after the New York's famous Coney Island, was nationally renowned in its time.

Here you could experience the stomach-tensing climb of the rollercoaster Thriller as it ratcheted up its big hills to pause briefly at the precipice before a screaming plunge down the far side. So too could be felt the violent twists and turns of Flying Turns, a ride whose operators carried smelling salts to revive riders who had fainted.

Music, whether it was the organ melodies of the merry-go-round Great American Racing Derby or the sounds of big-band orchestras in the great Dance Pavilion, floats through halcyon summer day memories of the park in the minds of countless older Clevelanders. Time took its toll however and the aging park was closed in 1969 and eventually razed to make way for housing.

Lake Shore Boulevard continues winding by old brick apartment buildings with wrought-iron terraces and into the mansion community of Bratenahl. Along the road here are a succession of lakeside walled estates, some stunning in size and grandeur, and many with elaborate gatehouses. The great lawns of the big houses on both sides of the road glow with the colors of autumn.

Lake Shore Boulevard emerges from Bratenahl and ends at I-90. At this juncture is the Gordon Park area of C.L.S.P., a large marina and parking area. The low shore here is thick with boulders piled into breakwalls. To the west the Cleveland skyline rises into view as the sun is in its evening plunge toward the lake.

From the park, I-90 west, known locally as Memorial Shoreway, heads downtown. Where I-90 makes a sharp left turn Ohio 2 continues along the shore passing Burke Lakefront Airport and to the East 9th Street exit and downtown Cleveland, a city a modern tale of urban fall and redemption.

Cleveland was a rough frontier outpost when founded by Moses Cleaveland in 1796. The "a" was dropped in 1831 so the name would fit on a newspaper masthead. In the 1800's Cleveland's growth as a major industrial center mirrored that of the growing, young country and by 1930 it was the nation's fifth largest city. Ships sailed into its lake port with iron ore and sailed out with refined steel. Smoke poured from its numerous factories, factories that beckoned immigrants to come and work and chase the American Dream.

In the 1920's Cleveland was a tapestry of over 50 nationalities with more foreign language daily newspapers than any city in the country. And its industrialists over the years had laid the foundations of a solid artistic and cultural community.

But the Great Depression dealt Cleveland's heavy industry-based economy a devastating blow and, other than a temporary World War II resurgence, the decline continued through the 1950's and 60's as factories closed their doors and relocated to the Sun Belt or overseas. Neighborhoods deteriorated, racial tensions twice exploded into riots in the 1960's, a section of the heavily polluted Cuyahoga River burst into flame in 1969, and tens of thousands of the city's residents fled to the suburbs.

Hastening the overall degeneration was a city government trying to navigate the currents of a changing world economy and urban decay while chained to the anchor of local politics and parochialism.

By the early 1970's Cleveland had become a butt of comedian's jokes , the "mistake-on-the-lake" whose downtown was dying, whose river caught on fire, and whose lake was so dirty nothing could live in it. Cleveland's collective psyche took a battering as well, and the title of a 1976 book by a longtime local newspaperman—*Cleveland: Confused City on a Seesaw*—gives an idea of the city's ebbing self-esteem. And the city's financial default in 1978, the first by a major city since the Depression, threw Cleveland into fiscal chaos.

But crisis has a way of bringing people together and local civic and business leaders, with nowhere to go but up, entered the 1980's determined to work together and reverse Cleveland's downward spiral. Its debts were paid off, towering new office buildings reshaped the downtown skyline, downtown shopping was revived with addition two major retail developments, and the renovation of Playhouse Square with its four historic and elegant theaters was completed.

Add to this the construction of a downtown baseball stadium and adjacent basketball arena, an awakening Warehouse District, and the evolvement of the once industrial banks of the Cuyahoga River into a major nightlife and entertainment center known as The Flats and the Cleveland of the mid-1970's and mid-1990's bore scant resemblance to each other both in appearance and in spirit.

Cleveland's makeover is immediately and strikingly apparent at the East 9th Street exit as the glass walls of the Rock and Roll Hall of Fame and Museum rise from the lakeshore. This pyramidal palace glitters in the evening twilight, a sight resplendent with the backdrop of sky in flaming sunset. The hall and museum, opened in 1995, houses decades of rock and roll history and memorabilia. Its existence here is at the end of a chain of events that began in the 1950's when Cleveland disc jockey Alan Freed coined the term "rock n' roll."

Adjacent to the rock hall is the Great Lakes Science Center, opened in 1996, and one of the largest hands-on science museums in the country with over 300 interactive exhibits and a six story dome housing a huge high-tech theater. Winding behind both buildings are the waterside walkways and boat basin of North Coast Harbor. Not a bad transformation for an area that a few years back was primarily a gravel stadium parking lot.

Just west of the science center stands old Municipal Stadium, silent and empty, and awaiting the wrecking ball. The Cleveland Indians moved out after the 1993 season and the historic park was scheduled to undergo a major renovation and continue to be the home of the Cleveland Browns and their passionate fans as it had been for 50 years.

But in 1995 city officials were blindsided by the team's owner who, despite previous vows that he would never move the team, signed a pact in secret to move the franchise to Baltimore. The National Football League, seeking to avoid lengthy and embarrassing litigation, promised the city a new team by 1999 but with one catch. The old park would have to go.

A new stadium will be built on the same site. The rubble of the old will be dumped offshore in Lake Erie becoming a fishing reef. The bricks and mortar of the old stadium will bring together fathers and sons to spend time fishing just as it once did to watch a game. And as night falls, the giant old stadium, an immense warehouse of memories for so many Clevelanders, looks almost haunted as it awaits its fate.

Chapter VI:

CLEVELAND TO LAKESIDE

From the rock hall, East 9th Street climbs from the lakeshore and into the downtown area. At the corner of St. Clair Avenue rises more glassy evidence of Cleveland's renaissance, Galleria, a two-story atrium mall with over 60 shops and restaurants.

Two blocks beyond Galleria, a right on Superior Avenue leads to the Cleveland Public Library with its ornate interior of wall murals, handcrafted wood, and marble staircases. The original 1930 facility is being enhanced by a $100 million expansion.

Superior Avenue continues west and emerges into the middle of Cleveland's heart, Public Square, a ten-acre commons platted by a surveyor with Moses Cleaveland's party 200 years ago. On a late October morning tall buildings shade the square's gardens and statues while the muffled and diesel-scented roar of engines, horns, and busses echoes. Small armies of pigeons busily patrol the grounds, at times disappearing in clouds of steam rising from grates while scattered lake gulls wing overhead. Men and women in suits hurry by, briefcases in hand, while others not so well dressed, and who call the square home, amble by.

Towering new office buildings front the square's southeast and northeast quadrants while at the northwest the Old Stone Church sits with the same quiet dignity it has since 1855. Over

10,000 people gathered in and around the church the morning of April 5, 1968 to hear a eulogy of Dr. Martin Luther King Jr. who was slain the day before. At the same time in speech in a hotel across the square a saddened Senator Robert F. Kennedy denounced the "mindless violence" that had taken the civil rights leader's life, little realizing his own life would meet a similar end two months later. Gracing the southwest corner of the square is Terminal Tower, a spire that reaches over 700 feet in the air. It was the tallest office building in the world outside of New York City and a source of immense civic pride when it rose over Cleveland in 1927. An enduring landmark, it has been both a beckon and a beacon for Clevelanders, a tower of strength unbowed by bad economic times or the slants of Lake Erie's storms.

The elaborate Union Terminal below the building was finished in 1929 capping off what had been a decade of tremendous growth for the city. On October 23rd the first passenger train rolled in and smiling railroad executives shook hands and posed for pictures. Six days later the stock market crashed and Cleveland would never be the same again. While the great passenger trains no longer rumble under Terminal Tower cars of the local light rail system (RTA) still do. And part of the old Union Terminal has been renovated into Tower City Center, a three-tiered complex of upscale shops, restaurants, and theaters. Outdoor balconies overlook the Cuyahoga River and Collision Bend, part of an oxbow in the serpentine river that meant gouged hulls to many a nineteenth century ship and still challenges the modern navigator.

From Public Square Superior Avenue courses west to West 9th Street and the cusp of the Cuyahoga River valley and the Detroit-Superior (Veteran's Memorial) Bridge. This elaborate double-decked bridge (the lower deck was for streetcars) was completed in 1918 and is nearing the completion of a major restoration. To the right a narrow road snakes down to the river and The Flats, once the industrial aorta of Cleveland.

The banks of the Cuyahoga once bristled with manufacturing and sooty smoke rising from the valley at times obscured Terminal Tower above. But then came the decline and the 1970's found this area to be a weedy and rusty wasteland, the river that caught on fire flowing past empty warehouses and shuttered factories. Other than a rough seaman's bar or two it was a place few ventured, especially at night.

But around 1980 developers began converting some of the old buildings into trendy taverns and restaurants, an effort that gained momentum and assumed a life of its own. Now scores of eateries and nightclubs line the river's banks in structures that at one time seemed to be prime candidates for the wrecking ball. Now on warm summer nights the valley swells with people while an army of pleasure boats plys the river. Ascending above the valley bottom are the steely skeletons of girder lift bridges, monuments to The Flats' industrial heritage. A total of eight majestic Flats bridges are illuminated after dark, colorful urban sculptures against the black night sky. Part of the upstream Cuyahoga is still a working river and during the day great ore freighters wind their way ever so carefully through the narrow river channel, behemoths in slow motion, and an impressive sight from a waterside establishment.

The tracks of the Waterfront Line of the RTA, Ohio's shortest rail line, runs through The Flats and travel between an area near the rock hall and Tower City Center. On this day a large tour group of senior citizens is riding the rails and seeing a city that in their lifetime has known peaks and valleys and is doggedly climbing a peak again. West 10th Street crawls along the east bank of the river and loops around to Center Street which crosses the Cuyahoga over short, red lift bridge to the west bank and the attractions on that side. Beneath the aqua painted steel work of the Main Avenue (Memorial Shoreway) Bridge that arcs high overhead, Main Avenue travels west up and out of the valley to West 25th Street. To the left about 100 feet is an access ramp to the Shoreway, Ohio 2 west, also US 6 and US 20 west.

As the Shoreway leaves downtown behind, Edgewater Park, the last of the six areas of C.L.S.P., appears on the right. A park since 1894, the lower area features a broad swimming beach and piers and breakwalls for fishing. The upper area crowns a high bluff with picnic areas and old pavilion. The bluff not only provides a fine view of the Cleveland skyline and the lake but also serves as a launching point for hang gliders.

Continuing west, the shoreway ends and becomes Clifton Boulevard, a broad avenue that rolls through an old residential Cleveland neighborhood of well-kept brick apartment buildings and stone houses. At West 117th Street is the Cleveland city limit and Lakewood, a suburb for over 100 years.

In addition to the above glimpse, Cleveland's cultural roots run deep. University Circle, a unique 500-acre enclave, is home to a university, eight museums including Art, Natural History, Health, and African-American, the Cleveland Playhouse, Severance Hall and the world-renowned Cleveland Orchestra, art galleries, theaters, numerous works of sculpture, and lagoons and gardens. The four restored theaters of Playhouse Square include The State with 3,400 seats and a 180-foot long Italian Renaissance lobby and the Palace Theater with 3,580 seats, a lavish three-story lobby, and dual marble staircases. Downtown is home to the Cleveland Indians, the Cleveland Cavaliers of the N.B.A., and the N.F.L.'s Cleveland Browns scheduled to return in 1999. Cleveland's zoo is one of the country's oldest and features over 3,300 animals. In addition Cleveland has a thick band of suburbs with many attractions of their own. And the city's rich ethnic heritage manifests itself with intact ethnic neighborhoods including Little Italy on the east side and with a variety of festivals year-round. For more information, call the Convention and Visitors Bureau of Greater Cleveland at 800-321-1004.

Clifton Boulevard rolls through Lakewood and to a bridge high above the Rocky River valley. To the left on the east side of the bridge a road slopes sharply down to the valley floor and the downriver segment of Rocky River Reservation, a miles-long park that meanders along the Rocky River. The Reservation is part of a 100-mile strand of river valley parkland known locally as the "Emerald Necklace" that encircles the Cleveland metro area. The eastern end of this winding esplanade that courses along four rivers emerges at the Chagrin River in Eastlake.

Here in this part of the Reservation are quiet riverside picnic grounds and trails shaded by tall trees. The Rocky River, dappled with leaves sauntering by in the slight current, is backdropped by a sheer valley wall.

Back on top, the bridge crosses over the valley to the community of Rocky River. The road, now Lake Road, a.k.a. US 6 passes by upscale shops and homes and comes to Bradstreet's Landing, a small park with an elevated, concrete fishing pier, a deck empty in a rising wind.

Lake Road continues along the lake to Bay Village and the Huntington Reservation, a metropark once the estate of Cleveland magnate John Huntington. Here a variety of deciduous trees shade lakeside grounds and walkways including a large ginko tree near the picnic shelter. The ginko, with its fan-shaped leaves, is the sole survivor of an ancient and once widespread family of Asian trees. Buddhist priests in China and Japan, who viewed it as sacred, preserved it over time, likely saving it from extinction.

On the shore rises a tall, yellow structure that looks like a lighthouse but is actually an old water tower that once pumped water from the lake to water the orchards of the estate. From the tower, 60 steps zig-zag to a thin and windswept beach below.

Across US 6 where the majority of the park's acres lie is a playhouse, an art and crafts center, and The Lake Erie Nature & Science Center. The center presents and promotes a variety of nature programs and has live reptiles and mammals on display including birds of prey, fox, deer, and a couple of pythons totaling 30 feet in length. The center, which was undergoing a major expansion as of this writing, is open seven days a week with no admission charge.

US 6 continues west to Avon Lake and Veterans Memorial Park, anchored to the unprotected apex of Avon Point, where the wind this day has sent the lake into whitecapped fury. The sound of waves slamming against the small and rocky beach is joined by the dry rattle of oak leaves clinging to their bankside trees and the laugh of a gull suspended in the gale above.

Avon Lake Cemetery is adjacent to the park where some of the town's first residents lie. A flat stone bears the grief of pioneer parents named Brown who laid their son Allen to rest on a frozen January day in 1842.

Here is one of our number
He was all in his bloom
He is called away by death

Huntington Metropark

And laid in his tomb
Although he is dead
He is a speaking to you
Although he is dead
He invites you to come
He is called away by death
And he is laid in his tomb
No more sighs nor groans
He feels no pain
Sickness can never wreck
His feeble frame again

Also along US 6 in Avon Lake is Miller Road Park and an adjacent lake access and the propeller from the tug the *Alva B*. Taking on water during the dark of a November storm in 1917, the tug's frightened crew headed for shore and for the lights that appeared to mean safe harbor. The glow they saw however was that of an amusement park once here and the ship went to Lake Erie's bottom. While the crew escaped, the propeller laid there for over 70 years until raised in 1989.

US 6 passes through Avon Lake which blends into Sheffield Lake and its several, small lakeside picnic grounds and on to the city of Lorain where it becomes Erie Street. A right on Colorado Street leads to Lakeside Landing, a large marina and park recently renovated and operated by the Lorain Port Authority. From the pier can be seen the rocky lake cliffs to the east and the homes that hunker on them. Columns of water explode upward as the waves slam into the unyielding shore.

From the walkway and benches on a grassy hill above the marina, the historic Lorain lighthouse can be seen through a forest of sailboat masts perched on a breakwall at the entrance to the harbor. The lights on the posts along the walkway are shaped like ships bells.

An ambitious Moravian missionary attempted a settlement here in 1787 where the Black River flows into Lake Erie but was sent packing by Delaware Indians. It wasn't until 1834 that a town named after the river was incorporated here, later to be called Lorain.

From the park, Erie Street crosses the Black River over a lift bridge to Lakeview Park, an older bluffside tract with a swimming beach and boardwalk where folks linger over lunch, some sharing their repast with noisy gulls. An expansive rose garden, started in 1934, adorns this park with hundreds of rose bushes of dozens of varieties planted in concentric circles. This garden has been put to bed for the winter by its caretakers and awaits a blanket of snow to sleep through the cold and gray days to come.

From Lorain railroad tracks escort US 6 west through the industrial section of Elyria to the historic harbor town of Vermilion, named for the red clay once used by Indians to make paint. The "V" in the town's name could also stand for Victorian as architecture of that era abounds here. The corner of US 6 and Main Street whispers history with old commercial buildings and a small town park with a red brick building. Public Comfort Station, the sign on the building says, built in 1912.

There's a definite seaside feel here as the hulls of power boats and tall masts of sailboats crowd the marinas and docks of the Vermilion River on its winding course through town. Riverside homes and cottages face the water.

From US 6 Main Street slopes north to the lake and to a 1909 stone mansion, home of the Inland Seas Maritime Museum, and a small, public beach. To the south, Main Street crosses railroad tracks into a bit of New England. Here can be found white picket-fenced homes, old churches, an opera house, and a stately town hall whose red brick walls rose in 1883. In fact the first settlers came here from New England in the 1790's. "Firelanders" they were called as they were granted this land by the federal government after the British had reduced their Connecticut homes and farms to ashes during the American Revolution.

Vermilion is also home to the Fish Festival in June and a Boat Regatta August. For more information, call the Vermilion Chamber of Commerce at 216-967-4477. The maritime museum is open daily. For more information call 216-967-3467.

US 6 leaves Vermilion passing the pink marble edifice of the town library. "Pink Georgia Marble to be exact, the librarian inside explains, "over 30 tons of it." A small lakeside park lies beyond the library. The road continues along the lake mixing simple, one room cottages with sprawling and expensive condominium developments, many still under construction.

Just before the city of Huron is Old Woman Creek Estuary and a nature center, a state preserve designated as a National Estuarine Research Reserve, a program to save and study the few remaining estuaries in the United States.

Legend has it that here in the 1750's an Indian maiden jumped in front of her French explorer lover who was being executed by members of her tribe and died by the same arrow. Her grief-stricken mother flung herself into the creek and drowned, thus Old Woman Creek.

A winding, hillside path at the preserve leads to a viewing platform where the waters of Old Woman Creek have widened into a broad estuary, its water lotus beds in late October decline.

The large embrace of the estuary filters out sediments and pollutants before its waters reach Lake Erie and holds the torrents of water sent by winter snowmelt or heavy rainstorms. Its nutrient-rich waters feed hundreds of species of migratory birds and over 40 kinds of fish. A bald eagle pair nest here having returned a number of springs in a row to their great nest on the western side of this wetland. The young they produce are adding to Ohio's tiny, but growing, bald eagle population. The generally young forest here, shadowed in places by soaring oaks along a hillside trail, is busy with migrating birds this day. Faded fall warblers hop from branch to branch feeding for their journey to the tropics while the haunting song of the elusive white-throated sparrow echoes.

How still it is here in the woods.
The trees Stand motionless, as if they did not dare
To stir, lest it should break the spell...
Sometimes a hawk screams or a woodpecker
Startle the stillness from its fixed mood
With his loud careless tap.
Sometimes I hear
The dreamy white-throat from some far off tree

Pipe slowly on the listening solitude,
His five pure notes succeeding pensively.
Archibald Lampman, *Solitude*

Old Woman Creek Estuary is open to the public 8 a.m. to 5 p.m. seven days a week. The nature center is open 1 to 5 p.m. Wednesday through Sunday.

US 6 continues to Huron where Tiffin Road leads to Nickel Plate Park, a swimming beach and park near where the Huron River, empties into Lake Erie. Across the grain elevator-lined river, Main Street winds along the river's west bank toward the lake, passing the Huron Boat Basin and Amphitheater and curves and becomes Cleveland Road. After a couple of blocks, a right on Center Street leads back to the shore and a quiet town park, a piece of ground with some history to it.

Here Christ Episcopal Church, built in 1839, faces the lake, its dignified red brick with white trim exterior will soon feel the blast of its 158th Lake Erie winter. The first white settlement in the Western Reserve was established here in 1790 and before that, French explorers built an outpost here in 1749.

A different kind of adventurer is here this day as a couple of windsurfers, taking advantage of the strong breeze, are slicing through the surf offshore, their black wet suits glinting in the sun. "My wife thinks I'm nuts but it's really not that dangerous," says one as he drags his board and sail ashore. "As long as you stay inside the breakwall and out of the big waves its pretty safe."

"This is really the best time of year to surf," says the other. "You don't get the all day wind like this in the summer and in the spring the water is too cold."

Huron is the Southernmost port on Lake Erie and has ample marina space downtown and a mile-long fishing pier. For more information, call the Huron Chamber of Commerce at 419-433-5700.

From the church, Ohio Street travels back to Cleveland Road which goes west out of town—there is an art deco style school building on Ohio just south of Cleveland Road. The road rejoins US 6 and travels to the Sheldon Marsh State Nature Preserve, a nearly 400-acre coastal wetland rich with a diversity of plant and animal life. Dean Sheldon was a Sandusky physician and visionary who bought part of this preserve in the early 1950's to save it from developers and manage it for the benefit of wildlife. Since some state maps still mark this place as "Sheldon's Folly," his efforts at the time must have been viewed with skepticism if not ridicule.

An old gate and wrought iron and stone fence front the entrance to the preserve through which once passed excited children on their way to the wonders of Cedar Point Amusement Park many years ago. The pounding of the lake on the roadway eventually forced construction of an alternate motor route and this grand entrance remains as a corridor to the wonders of nature.

Sheldon Marsh State Preserve and its trails are open daily from dawn to dusk.

Beyond Sheldon Marsh is an explosion of motels marking the present-day entrance to the enormously popular Cedar Point Amusement Park which draw visitors by the millions. The sandy peninsula of Cedar Point began drawing people in the 1830's to enjoy its fishing and swimming. The first roller coaster was built in 1892 and thrilled riders with speeds of up to 10 miles per hour.

During the first half of this century throngs of visitors came by land and by sea to Cedar Point. Then interest began to wane and by mid-1950's the aging park was ready to close. But the park was refurbished and new rides were added and it is now one of the world's outstanding amusement parks with a dozen roller coasters among its hundreds of attractions.

US 6 continues into the city of Sandusky. Wyandot Indians called this place "San-doos-tee" which meant "at the cold water." US 6 slants downtown and at Washington Street bumps into Washington Park, a square containing what is perhaps the prettiest public garden on Lake Erie. Its raised flower beds are classic Victorian with the logos of various community groups spelled out in flowers. Exotic trees and plants not native to Ohio and grown in a city greenhouse abound. And one of the more unique time/date services is here as the broad face of clock slants out of a flower bed. At the base the date is spelled out with plants changed daily by park workers.

To the south of the park is "The Boy With the Boot" fountain and the simple but elegant limestone exterior of the Erie County Courthouse built in 1874. Just to the west of the courthouse is the curve of the portico of a Neo-Classical post office building built in 1927, now a merry-go-round museum complete with a working carousel inside.

From Washington Park, Columbus Avenue travels north toward Sandusky Bay and to the Water Street Historic District. On the east and west blocks of Water Street stand the buildings of the original mercantile district of Sandusky built between 1835 and 1870. The open area between the blocks once teemed with life as the clip-clop of horse drawn wagons, the chugging of locomotives, and whistle blasts of steamers echoed as they converged on this spot to discharge passengers.

It is a far quieter place now. However the variety of Lake Erie island ferries and cruise ships bobbing at the docks at the foot of Columbus Street are evidence that this area relives its transportation hub glory days in the summer months.

Many of the historic buildings in the mercantile district and on Columbus Street have been restored. One of those buildings is the State Theater at the corner of West Water and Columbus streets, its 1929 elegance once again echoes with concerts and theater. Johnson Island and the peninsula of Cedar Point Amusement Park, can be seen from the Jackson Street Pier, both wrapped ever so slightly in an Indian Summer haze. Some of the park's fleet of roller coasters can be seen, the spider web of wooden trestles of the coasters mixing with the brightly painted steel of the modern ones. In the summer the shrieks of excited riders floats across the water.

In July, 1897 a gigantic waterspout awed crowds of onlookers here. As recorded in the (Cleveland) *Marine Record* it lasted nearly 20 minutes and "took up large quantities of water and whirled it through the air at terrific rate of speed. The dimensions reached by the waterspout were approximately 25 feet in diameter and reached a height of several thousand feet. It was an awe-inspiring sight to witness the fall of the immense column of water when it broke away from the influence of the whirlwind."

Sandusky is home to one of the largest collections of limestone buildings in Ohio and has a downtown architectural tour with 50 stops. It also hosts the Erie County Fair in August. For more information, call the Erie County Convention and Visitors Bureau at 419-625-2984 or 800-255-ERIE. For more information on Cedar Point Amusement Park and its rides, legendary swimming beach, RV campground and the historic Hotel Breakers built around the turn of the century, call the park at 419-627-2350.

US 6 travels west to the edge of town to the intersection of Venice Road. Here is a marker that tells of Fort Sandusky. This was a lonely outpost in 1754 when the French built a small fort here at the beginning of their war against England. Abandoned in 1759, the British built a more solid fort in 1760. Three years later a sergeant was planting vegetables in the garden on a warm May day when some angry Indians came to call, Indians taking a stand against white encroachment under the leadership of Chief Pontiac. Most of the whites were killed in the flurry that followed and the fort was plundered and burned.

The fort's commander was captured and taken to Detroit where he expected to be killed. However an old squaw who had recently lost her husband wanted him as a substitute and he was spared. He later escaped and lived to tell what happened here over 230 years ago.

Venice Road continues west from the marker, bracketed by Sandusky Bay on one side and wetlands on the other, to the hamlet of Bay View, a town literally at the end of the road. Ohio 269 once passed through this place and over the bay. However a boating accident damaged part of the long, low, bay bridge and the state declined to repair it rerouting the road over the nearby Thomas A. Edison Memorial Bridge. This brought to an end much of the traffic passing through Bay View, isolating the town and its fine view of Sandusky Bay. The former bridge just might be one of the world's longest unplanned fishing piers.

A man on the pier wearing a hat that says *Eat...Sleep...Go Fishing* is trying his luck this day. "A couple of perch for dinner would be nice, he says as he casts into the choppy water, "but this wind sure isn't helping."

He then talks about the loss of the bridge. "A lot of people said this town would die but that didn't happen. Yeah, things slowed down but people still stop here. They come here to fish and go to the Angry Trout (restaurant) to eat," he observes. "I really don't miss the bridge. I come here to fish all the time."

From Bay View, Martin's Point Road jogs to Ohio 2 west which leads to the Edison Bridge and its graceful arch over Sandusky Bay, a bridge sometimes closed when a winter's howl makes it too dangerous to cross.

On the far side of the bridge is Ohio 269 north and an exit to Bay Shore Road which travels east to explore the Marblehead Peninsula, a rocky arm of land reaching into the lake and rich in history and beauty. The road passes cottages and low fields thick with feeding Canada geese and rises sharply to the Dempsey Sandusky Bay Fishing Access, a large area with a sweeping view of Sandusky Bay and the city of the same name on its distant shore. Over a hill beyond the access, Bay Shore Road curves to the right. After about a mile is a small, gravel parking lot and a marker on the right; First Battle Site. The first War of 1812 battle on Ohio soil was fought here on September 29, 1812 when about 60 Americans and 130 Indians clashed. The main body of Americans escaped by boat to Cedar Point returning later to rescue the others who had holed up in a cabin.

From the marker, a path slopes under a willow tree and over a footbridge to a small cemetery where a weathered stone lists the names of the eight Americans who died that late September day. Also in this plot is a small marker bearing the name of a soldier of the American Revolution, Equilla Puntney, also spelled Aquilla Puntenney, who apparently is buried here.

A few yards up the road on the left is the 1820 stone house of Benajah Wolcott, one of the first settlers of the peninsula and the first keeper of the Marblehead Lighthouse. Some period furniture can be seen through its old windows. A short hop up the road from the Wolcott house on the right lies the road to Johnson Island and its self-operated toll gate. While the island is privately owned, there is parking, displays, and a cemetery where once stood a prison for Confederate soldiers during the Civil War.

The first unwilling Southerners came in 1862, the prison eventually becoming a facility for officers only with an occasional private mixed in by mistake. Each day ended as it began with a roll call as the prisoners were free to move about the stockade during the day.

Many walked these frozen and icebound island grounds in the winter numbed by cold they had never before felt and heavy with worry about loved ones back home. They were imprisoned not only by walls but by a culture and climate so different from their own. Their primary enemy being boredom, the prisoners played baseball, taught each other foreign languages, formed debate teams, and even formed a theatrical group called The Rebel Thespians performing original material.

Life wasn't too bad for the rebels on the whole and they ate about as well as did a Union soldier in the field. However when news of the brutality and starvation taking place in Confederate P.O.W. camps reached the North, the War Department cut the prisoner's rations in half in 1864, forcing them to eat rats to supplement their diets.

More than 2800 Confederates had been imprisoned on Johnson Island when war came to an end the following spring. Over 200 did not make the return trip south having died from disease, wounds, or execution. Their white marble gravestones slope toward the bay where the late afternoon sun warms a bronze statue of a Confederate soldier standing guard over these grounds. All the graves here are unadorned save for one, that of a lieutenant from the Third Texas Calvary where silk flowers brighten the ground under the shade of an aged locust tree.

Bay Shore Road continues east, "around the horn" as it's known locally then curves north, becoming Ohio 163 and toward the village of Marblehead. Outside of town is Lake Pointe Park, a small lakeside picnic ground. From here the road swings back to the west and to Lighthouse Drive which leads to the historic Marblehead Lighthouse.

The beam of this light has pierced the night since 1822 making it the oldest operating lighthouse on all the Great Lakes and a tribute to the skill of its builders. Its white tower gleams against an ice blue sky this last October day, unbowed by the hurls of nearly two centuries of Lake Erie's storms, storms that at times slam this rocky point with 15-foot waves.

A red, wrought iron railing and roof cap this elegant spire. To the north, Kelleys and South Bass Islands rise from the lake, the 352-foot tall granite column of Perry's Victory Memorial easily landmarks the latter.

Benajah Wolcott hauled whale oil up the lighthouse's 85-foot prominence to fuel the lamp's 13 wicks until he fell victim to a cholera epidemic. Several cholera epidemics swept over the Marblehead Peninsula, including one in 1834 that started when dead cholera victims were tossed off a passing ship. Unwary Marblehead residents dragged them ashore to give them a proper burial, an act of charity with deadly consequences.

The road continues west becoming Main Street and to Marblehead village, its preserved center, with shops and art galleries, could easily be mistaken for one in New Hampshire or Vermont. In front of an 1893 former schoolhouse that now houses shops is an old hand-operated water pump, Marblehead's first public water supply.

The 160-year old Marblehead quarry is still in operation here and a conveyor carrying stone arcs over Main Street to a dock on the lake. The unique habitat of the old quarries provides one of the world's only three homes to the lakeside daisy, Ohio's rarest plant, which blooms in May.

It was off Marblehead in 1874 that the schooner *Consuelo*, its load of stone shifting in its hold, foundered in a gale drowning most of the crew except for two who clung to the ship's spars for life. Captain Lucien Clemons and his two brothers set out in an open boat to rescue the sailors.

Despite the raging seas, they reached the two men and pulled them aboard and a passing tug towed the exhausted group to Kelley's Island. Captain Clemons and his brothers were awarded gold medals for their bravery by the United States government, the first ever awarded for the rescue of shipwrecked persons.

In 1876 the Marblehead life saving station was established

and Captain Clemons was named as its first keeper, a position he held for 21 years. An 1899 account described him as living "a life of retirement and ease within the sound of the dashing billows he has so often braved." As Main Street ascends from Marblehead's business district, Perry Street goes right to Elliot Street which winds toward the lake and the community of Lakeside.

Marblehead town and peninsula are host to a variety of events April through October including lighthouse tours. For more information, call The Peninsula Chamber of Commerce at 419-798-9777 or Ottawa County Visitors Bureau at 800-441-1271.

Passing through the gates of Lakeside is to leave one world behind and enter another. Time seems to have forgotten this enchanting place of old homes, shops, and churches, said to be one of the few remaining chautauquas in the world.

In 1869 Alexander Clemons of Marblehead, father of Lucien Clemons, shared with a group of 250 picnicking Methodists here his vision of a place where natural beauty would enhance spiritual and cultural growth. The Lakeside Company had formed by 1873 which gave birth to this refuge.

Lakeside maintains its tradition of cultural and spiritual nourishment with summertime conferences, lectures, and symphonies. The yellow and white frame of the historic Hotel Lakeside arises on the lake, closed for the season, its Victorian charm little changed from the days when horse and buggy tied up at its doors when it opened 120 years ago. A honeymooning couple can still be brushed by a soft lake breeze while sitting in a white, wicker chair on the grand front porch.

A town park adjacent to the hotel has oak-shaded gazebos, shuffleboard courts, and a waterside Victorian pavilion. An exact replica of the original, its dock stretches well into the lake and recalls the days when vacationers poured from passenger ships.

The hilly streets here are lined with pin-neat cottages and homes, most shuttered for the long wait when the light of spring melts the frosting of winter off this picturesque village. Few people are seen on the windswept streets this bright but quiet day as a cat peers warily from behind a tree, a far different pace from its summer hum.

For more information on Lakeside activities and the hotel, call the Lakeside Association at 419-798-4461 or Ottawa County Visitors Bureau at 800-441-1271.

Chapter VII:

LAKESIDE TO THE DETROIT RIVER

From Lakeside's west gate, North Shore Boulevard passes the Mazurik Access Area, a boat access with a long fishing pier. The road rejoins Ohio 163 which travels to Ohio 269 and north to East Harbor State Park. The park was once of part the northern edge of the Great Black Swamp, an enormous area of marshland and sand ridges darkened in places by towering trees. The swamp swept from the lakeshore across Northwest Ohio to near present-day Fort Wayne, Indiana.

East Harbor today is water-wrapped land and a place for the aquaphile with boating, fishing and wetlands. The sandy swimming beach on the lake replaced a much broader beach once located a few hundred yards to the south. That beach was swept into memory by a ferocious winter storm in 1972 when the lake level brimmed near a record high.

On the dike where the beach used to be is now a lakeside picnic ground. This combined with hundreds of tables located along the roads and broad boulevards of the park make East Harbor a picnickers' paradise.

East Harbor State Park features 570 campsites, none with electrical hook-ups, showers/flush toilets, and group camping. For more information, call the park at 419-734-4424.

Back to Ohio 163, the road heads west to Ohio 53 which jogs north to course the eastern side of Catawba Island. This "island" is actually a peninsula as it is connected to the mainland by a thread of land on its western side. On the left after a half-mile is East Wine Cellar Road and the Mon Ami Restaurant and Historic Winery.

Even the teetotaller will appreciate the beauty of this 1872 winery, a sturdy three-story stone building trimmed with black shutters. The four to six-foot thick limestone blocks used in its construction descend two stories below ground level where vaulted cellars store giant casks of wine. What was started as a simple cooperative winery by European immigrants now produces 26 varieties of wines.

From the winery, Ohio 53 continues up the eastern side of Catawba Island passing by an almost continuous succession of marinas and watercraft related businesses, and ends at Catawba's northern tip. This unprotected point is feeling the fury of a southwestern gale this day as the forces of summer and winter engage in their annual battle. Robust after its journey across open waters, the wind drowns out all sound save for the pummeling of the surf.

Great, gray waves slam against an island ferry pier blasting geysers of water high into the air. Passengers and freight, despite the torment of the lake, await the next ferry and a short but lurching crossing to South Bass Island and Put-in-Bay.

Nay, Wind, I hear you, desperate brother, in your might
Whistle and howl; I shall not tarry long,
And though the day be blind and fierce, the night
Be dense and wild, I still am glad and strong
To meet you face to face; through all your gust and drifting
With brow held high, my joyous hands uplifting
I cry you song for song.

Archibald Lampman, *Storm*

CR 30 rides down the west side of Catawba Island to Moore's Road and Catawba Island State Park, one of three parks known collectively as Lake Erie Islands State Park. This park is a day-use place with picnic grounds, boat launch, and fishing pier. Rolling surf drenches the pier and its shelter house. Gulls pluck their lunch from the glistening water as it washes over the pier's concrete deck as the wind continues to roar.

A different sort of roar swept over this shore on the bright and blue noon of September 10, 1813 when the British fleet from Amherstburg and Commodore Perry's fleet that had been docked at Put-in Bay met in Battle of Lake Erie in the waters near South Bass Island. The two fleets hammered each other with their heavy cannons at close range and decks flowed red with blood while ships masts fell like trees in a windstorm. The thunder of the cannons echoed around the lake and the villagers of Cleveland rushed headlong to the shore to try to guess which side was winning.

A couple of hours into the battle Perry transferred his flag from his heavily damaged flagship *Lawrence* to the *Niagara* and the fight raged on, the smoke from the cannons blotting out the sun. Shortly after that a shift in the wind allowed him to sail his warships through the heart of the outnumbered and outgunned British fleet while his cannons blazed away.

Around 3 p.m. a white handkerchief was waved from the British flagship *Detroit* and the great guns on both sides fell silent. Silent too were the dead that littered the decks of British and American warships.

It was the first time in history a British fleet had been defeated and captured intact. And Perry's account to his superiors of the battle, "We have met the enemy and they are ours. Two ships, two brigs, one schooner, one sloop," remains legendary in the annals of military discourse today. Within a month the British were swept from the Western Lake Erie theater at the Battle of Thames. Never again would the waters of Lake Erie serve as a killing field.

Lake Erie Islands State Park also include Kelleys Island State Park with 129 campsites, none with electrical hookups, and showers/flush toilets. The park also features swimming, Lake Erie and inland lake fishing, and the opportunity to view 12,000-year old glacial grooves. For more information, call the park at 419-746-2546. South Bass Island State Park has 132 sites in a blufftop campground, none with electrical hookups, and showers/vault toilets. Some sites are considered cliffside sites with a spectacular view and a small number of cabins are rented on a lottery basis only. For more information, call the park at 419-285-2112.

CR 30 continues south and leaves to the left while Sand Road follows the lake over a rocky ridge to Ohio 163 and Port Clinton. Here is a lakeside community in the truest sense of the word where even the parking lots of fast food restaurants afford a fine view of the lake.

Ohio 163, a.k.a. Perry Street, promenades along the shore past the picnic grounds and swimming beach of Lakeview Park through clouds of wind-whipped sand and a barren shoreline, its water pushed away by the power of the wind this day. Giant pumps stand sentinel, ready to repel the invading lake back when a north wind sends it marching over the shore. Mansions face the lake along the road as it enters the historic downtown area, a peek through the window of time.

At Perry and Madison streets stands the Island House Hotel, built in 1886, its faded red brick accented by white wooden shutters and woodwork supporting an awning around the first floor. Inside, the muted glow of brass chandeliers casts the old lobby with a 19th century ambiance. Thirty-seven rooms, all recently renovated and with period decor, await the traveler who wants to check into a bygone era.

A couple of blocks south on Madison Street is the Ottawa County Courthouse, a Romanesque castle of a building built in 1899. An ornate clock tower gives the correct time in all four directions. Inside the building's west entrance is a wall mural of Commodore Perry transferring his flag at the height of the Battle of Lake Erie.

The Portage River provides the northern border of downtown and a sea smell surrounds the docks of the numerous Lake Erie island ferries and marinas lining the river's bank. Where Madison Street ends at the river is an old fish house, the Port Clinton Fish Company. Inside, workers dump shovelfuls of ice over cases of freshly packed fish.

"This has been a fish house since the 1920's," said the clerk peering over a glass display case of fish for sale, chilling on a bed of ice. "Of course it had to close in the 50's and 60's when the lake got so bad. Business is pretty good now but it always could be better. A lot of people who go the islands or out in boats bring their fish for us to clean. We see a lot of the same folks."

Good news for those fishermen and women descended on Port Clinton in late June, 1996 when great clouds of mayflies rolled in from the lake for the first time since the 1950's. The wispy insect typically spends the first two years of its life as an egg at lake's bottom before rising from the water to take wing, mate, and die, usually all in the same day.

They descended on the city by the millions coating windows and street lights before their carcasses piled up on the ground to be swept into piles and hauled away in garbage bags. Downtown was temporarily darkened as street lights were turned off to discourage the invading hordes.

But their return in such numbers after nearly a 40-year absence meant that the oxygen level at lake Erie's bottom, which once was so seriously depleted by pollution, was continuing to improve. And during their return the surface of Lake Erie swirled as fish eagerly feasted on the delicate but tasty mayfly.

Fishing is to the Port Clinton economy what tomatoes are to the economic health of Leamington, Ontario or grapes are to North East, Pa. This town that claims the title "Walleye Capital of the World" pays homage to that gamefish by lowering a large papier-mache walleye at midnight on New Year's Eve. Plenty of equipment dealers and charter operators are here for those seeking to harvest the rich fishing grounds of the lake's central and western basins. For the Lake Erie worshipper, Port Clinton is truly a mecca.

Port Clinton provides a jumping-off point for the enormously popular Lake Erie Islands that offer everything from rollicking night life to quiet beaches. For those planning an overnight stay, reservations made well in advance are recommended. For lodging availability, call 800-441-1271 or 419-734-1818. As well as summer events, Port Clinton offers year-round activities. For more information, call the Ottawa County Visitors Bureau at 800-441-1271.

Ohio 163 crosses the Portage River over an historic drawbridge and continues along the lake passing blue shrink-wrapped yachts to Lake Shore Road and right. Lake Shore emerges onto Ohio 2 at Camp Perry, a National Guard camp and scene of national rifle matches in the summer. The sounds of war once roared just beyond the camp at the Erie Proving Ground, a place where tanks and guns were tested by the over 5,000 personnel stationed here during World War II. Closed in 1967, it is now a considerably more quiet industrial park.

As Ohio 2 squeezes from four lanes into two, the massive cooling tower of a nuclear power plant looms on the horizon with clouds of steam roiling from its opening, stark white against the blue northern sky. The legs supporting this massive concrete superstructure look too spindly as water cascades from the tower's inside walls to the base.

Ohio 2 continues flat along the lake past fertile farmland on the south and rich wetland to the north over a low bridge to the Turtle Creek Access Area. A great blue heron searches the shallow waters here before flapping its massive wings in startled flight while willow trees and marsh grasses, in the process of turning from summer green to autumn yellow, sway in the wind.

From Turtle Creek, it's a short hop to the beaches of Crane Creek State Park and adjacent Magee Marsh Wildlife Area, the same road serves as entrance to both. Magee Marsh is an avian paradise where more than 300 species of birds can be seen during the year ranging from the tiny hummingbird to the magnificent bald eagle. One species that isn't seen is cranes as the early arrivers who named Crane Creek mistook herons and egrets for cranes. A long and winding lane leads from the highway through Magee Marsh, wetlands that teem with waterfowl in the warm months, and to the lake. This place is a virtual maternity ward of Canada geese in the spring as thousands of goslings scamper about under their parent's watchful eyes. Most are gone as October winds down, bound for warmer climes, to return next spring in a ritual as timeless as the ages. Warblers swarm this place during spring migration to rest before continuing their northern journey from Central and South America. A half-mile long boardwalk into Magee Marsh gives spring birdwatchers the chance to enter the diminutive warbler's world and marvel at their exotic colors.

Orioles, tanagers, and buntings add to the feathered rainbow that peaks in mid-May here. Many consider Magee Marsh to be the premier bird-watching place in the Midwest.

Along the lake's edge is the sandy beach and cottonwood-shaded picnic grounds of the state park. The shells of the tiny zebra mussel lay in piles on the beach. This recent European invader to the lake has been a pest clogging water intake lines, coating boat hulls, and may have ecological consequences that only the passage of time will reveal. But the filtering effect of the feeding of the millions of these shellfish has brought a clarity to Lake Erie's waters not seen in decades. This area, also once part of the Great Black Swamp, was spared from drainage and development last century by wealthy waterfowl hunters and fishermen who bought the land for private preserves. It is original wilderness in a region of the country that has virtually none. The state and federal government began buying back some it back in the 1950's and now over 8,000 acres are in the public domain here and in adjacent wildlife refuges.

One of those refuges is the Ottawa National Wildlife Refuge, just beyond Magee Marsh, whose skies darken with great flights of waterfowl during migratory seasons. Gulls, preparing to face another winter, line the sun-warmed ribbon of blacktop that leads to the refuge's trailhead this day. In succession they lift, ever so briefly, allowing vehicles to pass underneath before floating back to the balmy pavement.

Magee Marsh Wildlife Area also has the Sportsmen's Migratory Bird Center with wildlife displays and information and a three-story observation tower. For more information, call the marsh at 419-898-0960. Crane Creek State Park is a day-use area with swimming and picnic facilities. For more information, call the park at 419-898-2495. The Ottawa National Wildlife Refuge has a visitor center and maintains several trails for bird and waterfowl watching. For more information, call the refuge at 419-898-0014. All the above areas are open dawn to dusk year-round.

The busy highway that is Ohio 2 continues and where it bends back to the west after a northerly jog is the Metzger Marsh Wildlife Area. A road abuts a long marina channel here and ends at the lake and a long fishing pier. Mankind's understanding and appreciation of the importance of wetlands is in

Catawba Island

Ottawa National Wildlife Refuge

further evidence here as a wetland restoration project is taking place to recover nearly 1,000 acres of marsh. Once drained and converted to farmland, the lake's years of battering took its toll on the protective dikes until all were breached by 1952.

Beyond Metzger Marsh on Ohio 2, Decant Road goes north and ends at Cedar Point Road which borders the national wildlife refuge of the same name. Part of Southwestern Lake Erie's vast wetland territory, this area stretches to the lake flapjack flat in marked contrast to the bluffs and cliffs that soar over parts of the lake's eastern and central shores.

Going west on Cedar Point Road, cabins and golf course bunkers suddenly sprout out of the wetlands marking one of the state's newest parks, Maumee Bay State Park. The park's 1,400 acres include Maumee Bay and inland lake swimming beaches and a large, modern resort lodge where the Michigan shore appears to the north cloaked in a slight haze. Tall grasses move to the gusts of this day in mimic of a windswept day on the Great Plains in this open park of prairies, meadows, and small trees.

A two-mile boardwalk completed in 1992 that snakes through a marsh and wet woods is an avenue for those seeking a close wetlands encounter. The interpretive stops and observation tower and blind enhance the journey.

Maumee Bay State Park features 256 campsites, all with electrical hookups, showers/flush toilets, winter sports, and a year-round nature center. For more information, call 419-836-7758. For lodge reservations, call 800-282-7275.

A soldier named Samuel R. Brown spent a long night near here in 1813. Dispatched with a party from Fort Meigs up the Maumee River to deliver a letter to another post "we descended the Miami (Maumee River) in a canoe and at sun set had just reached the bay which like that of Sandusky has every appearance of a lake—it soon became dark and windy...It was about midnight when we landed; we were completely lost...We therefore hauled up our canoe and concealed ourselves in the grass till morning. My comrades slept soundly; as for me, it was the first time I had been exposed to the tomahawk, and every rustling I heard I fancied it was caused by the footsteps of a savage—my eyes never closed *that night.*

Brown's woes continued. "At the dawn of the day we repaired to the beach and found our canoe completely filled by the dashing of the surf. We had left everything in the canoe but our musket, (we had but one) our ammunition and provisions were completely soaked. Here we were, in Indian country with nothing to defend ourselves with but an ax and a musket which could not be discharged."

Samuel Brown went on to survive his ordeal and penned his memoirs in 1814.

Cedar Point Road goes on to the Toledo suburb of Oregon where Stadium Road heads north to Bay Shore Road and the lake. Along this final few miles of southern Lake Erie road is a small town park and the Maumee Bay Bay Shore Access, a small access in the shadow of a large power plant. The cove here has been swept of water by the wind setting the table for thousands of gulls feeding on the mud flat, their cries piercing the background hum of the plant's turbines.

Bay Shore Road curves beyond the power plant and goes south, its name changing to Otter Creek Road, and to Consaul Street. Consaul goes east to Birmingham, Toledo's Hungarian neighborhood. The neighborhood was so named in the 19th century due to its similarity to Birmingham, England and its great foundries that poured out smoke, soot, and steel.

A casting company built a plant here in 1890 and transferred experienced Hungarian workers from its factory in Cleveland. They in turn sent letters across the ocean to family and friends who left behind village and farm to become part of the Industrial Revolution sweeping through Toledo. By the early 1900's Birmingham had become a distinctly Hungarian enclave.

The newcomers worked hard and built a community where the sounds of the Hungarian language floated from front porches on warm summer nights. While Hungarians have since dispersed to all parts of Toledo, Birmingham retains its ethnic identity fed by the deep roots planted over a century ago.

The twin steeples of St. Stephens Church and the salmon-colored statue of its namesake grace Consaul Street. A step through the doorway of the old National Bakery on Whittemore

Street is a slip through the window of time. And the legendary Tony Packo's Cafe, made famous by Toledo-born Jamie Farr's Corporal Klinger character on the TV series MASH, anchors the corner of Consaul and Front streets.

From Tony Packo's, Front Street courses south along the Maumee River over I-280 and to Main Street. A right on Main Street leads toward the river and on the left just before the bridge is International Park. Here flags from 22 countries curve around a boat basin and the park affords a fine view of downtown Toledo.

To the north are the graceful arches of an historic drawbridge, built in 1914, and since named in honor of Dr. Martin Luther King Jr. It's the last of four bridges on this site. The first bridge here charged a penny per hog, two cents per person, and a dime per horse to cross. South up the river and high in the air can be seen the Anthony Wayne Bridge and its 200-foot tall towers. It was one of the longest suspension bridges in the world when it opened in 1931.

Toledo became a city in 1837 when the rival, riverside villages of Port Lawrence and Vistula merged. Settlement of the area had been delayed by the barrier of the Great Black Swamp and the lowland city's early days were marked by malaria, floods, and the nickname "Frogtown." Area newspapers teased the city by printing tales of horses and buggies sinking into the mud and out of sight. A colorful tile mosaic of a frog on the ground floor of the century-old Lucas County Courthouse harkens to those days.

Toledo grew steadily as an industrial and shipping center during the latter half of the 1800's and for a time local leaders were confident it was destined to become "the future great city of the Midwest." But the country continued to bulge westward and Chicago became the industrial and economic capitol of middle America. By 1900, Toledo was a major but secondary Great Lakes city, a good place to earn a living and raise a family.

The city had become a center of glassmaking with several glass plants turning out everything from window glass to ornate chandeliers. A machine invented here in 1901 that made light bulbs and glass bottles replaced the hand-blown method.

This revolutionized the industry and led to Toledo being dubbed "The Glass City." And the substantial endowments of one of those glass pioneers, Edward Drummond Libbey, led to the establishment of the world-class Toledo Museum of Art.

The growth continued and through the first few decades of the 1900's Toledo's story mirrored that of its sister cities of Cleveland and Buffalo; that of a burgeoning manufacturing center powered substantially by waves of immigrants building new lives in a new land. The 1920's saw the Toledo skyline grow with the construction of a number of office buildings and hotels and by 1930 the city's population neared 300,000. Then came the Great Depression and Toledo, like Cleveland and Buffalo, was brought to its knees.

Banks failed, factories closed, and unemployment hovered as high as 50% during those dark years. And a series of violent labor disputes that drew national attention culminated in 1934 when the Ohio National Guard fired into a crowd of angry strikers at an auto parts plant, killing two and wounding a number of others.

The second half of that decade saw the infusion of New Deal programs and money as Toledo slowly emerged from its economic stupor. Legacies of the New Deal years include the art deco downtown branch of the public library with its unique interior glass murals, Gothic architecture buildings at the University of Toledo, and the stone buildings and winding walkways of the Toledo Zoo.

Like the rest of the country, World War II put Toledo back to work. The four-wheel drive Jeep became the workhorse of the Army and hundreds of thousands of them rolled out of Toledo's assembly plant.

The postwar years saw the city remain relatively static in terms of growth, a medium-sized, northern industrial city coping with the shift of capital and population to other parts of the country. By the late 1970's Summit Street, Toledo's downtown avenue along the Maumee River, had degenerated into a row of deteriorating buildings and weedy, gravel parking lots and was sorely in need of a makeover.

The King Bridge crosses the river (Main Street becomes Cherry Street) and intersects with Summit Street on the west side. To the south, the skywalk-spanned Summit Street bears scant resemblance to its past with the construction in recent years of office buildings, corporate headquarters, hotels, and a convention center. At Summit and Adams streets is the Center of Science and Industry (C.O.S.I.), a hands-on learning and science museum housed in a glassy, multilevel building. The structure was once a festival marketplace that failed and the museum has brought it back to life.

At the intersection of Summit and Jefferson streets, Jefferson Street slopes toward the river and ends at Water Street, Toledo's oldest street. Here is Promenade Park, a grassy, riverside spread and gathering place for summer festivals and concerts and due to be enlarged with the razing of the Federal Building above.

On the park's northern edge, the towering smokestacks of the former Water Street Station point into a blue November sky. Built in 1896, the Romanesque Revival structure with its massive arched windows once housed giant coal burning generators that provided electricity to downtown buildings and trolley cars. From Promenade Park a riverside walkway extends north, passing by C.O.S.I., plazas and fountains, and ending at a Great Lakes nautical display under the King Bridge.

From the park Water Street jogs south and back to Summit Street and Monroe Street. A block south is Washington Street and left turn travels over an old counterweight lift bridge. The waterway underneath was once the northern terminus of the Miami and Erie Canal. On the other side of the bridge the new corporate headquarters of Owens-Corning brightens riverside land that was, until recently, crumbling brick buildings and gravel parking lots.

From Owens-Corning, Ottawa Street travels south along the old canal to the former Oliver House, a pretty Greek Revival structure and Toledo's finest hotel when it was built in 1859. Renovated after sitting empty for many years, the old inn now houses a restaurant and microbrewery.

Just beyond the Oliver House, Oliver Street goes right and back to Summit Street and north. Between Monroe and Jefferson streets on the right is Fort Industry Square, a commercial row with some of the oldest buildings in Toledo.

Summit Street continues north along the river and out of

the downtown area, passing under I-280 (alternate route to Michigan is I-280 north to I-75 north). After passing through old residential neighborhoods, the road passes by a lowland area since converted into golf courses. It was in this once swampy area that Toledo's minor league baseball team played a hundred years ago earning the nickname the Mud Hens, a moniker that sticks today.

Summit Street passes through Point Place, a residential neighborhood forced to build dikes in the early 1970's after high lake levels sent the waters of Maumee Bay rolling through its streets and homes. The road continues crossing a low bridge spanning the Ottawa River and into the state of Michigan before merging onto I-75 north.

Toledo is home to the Toledo Museum of Art with collections that span the spectrum of time and which is virtually the only major museum in the country with no admission charge. In addition there is C.O.S.I. and the museum ship Willis B. Boyer downtown, a firefighters museum in West Toledo, the 1830's Wolcott House Museum and complex of historical buildings in suburban Maumee, and the reconstructed War of 1812 Fort Meigs, the largest walled fort in the country, in suburban Perrysburg. The Toledo Zoo continues to expand and is home to over 3,000 animals representing over 500 species as well as special exhibits and interactive displays. The Toledo Mud Hens play Triple A ball in the summer, the Toledo Storm plays minor league hockey in the winter, and the University of Toledo hosts Division I sports. For more information call the Greater Toledo Convention and Visitors Bureau at 800-243-4667.

From Toledo north along Lake Erie, there is no continuous lakeshore road and little public access between Toledo and Monroe, Michigan, an area that is a blend of marsh and lowland cottages and homes. The colors of November are in command now and the silhouettes of barren trees bow over the tawny and chestnut land.

The quiet hamlet of Luna Pier is off Exit 6 of I-75. Here is a town park with a long fishing pier that curls into the lake. A solid concrete breakwall lines the shore here, a wall that takes a battering when a northeast gale roaring down Lake Erie's 240-mile southwestern slant rapidly piles up lake water. A few miles north of Luna Pier on I-75 is a rest area and Michigan Welcome Center with maps and travel information. At Exit 14 in Monroe, Elm Avenue passes under the interstate and to the War of 1812 Battle of Frenchtown historic site and visitors center. A late 1700's settlement here was dubbed Frenchtown for the French-Canadian families that had drifted down from Detroit after the Revolution to live on the river. The wild grapes that seemed to be growing everywhere led them to name the stream *Riviere Aux Raisins,* or River Raisin.

On an icy January dawn in 1813 American forces camping here were just rubbing reveille from their eyes when they were attacked by a British and Indian force from Amherstburg. The battle quickly turned into a rout and the Americans were swept into a disorganized retreat across the frozen river and back toward Ohio. The British returned to Amherstburg with their wounded telling wounded American prisoners they would return for them later.

Before any such party came, a band of Potawatomis returned to massacre and scalp the survivors. The Indians were seeking revenge for atrocities by American soldiers at Tippecanoe earlier in the war.

The news of the defeat, and in particular of the post-battle slaughter, crackled through Western Lake Erie theater and came to be known as the River Raisin Massacre. In February a British soldier at Amherstburg wrote of the event "Be assured we have not heard the last of this shameful transaction." His words proved to be prophetic as "Remember the Raisin" became a rallying cry that spirited American troops to eventual victory at the Battle of the Thames later that year.

West from the battlefield, East Elm Avenue travels along the River Raisin to downtown and Monroe Street (M-125) where rises a statue of a onetime local resident who became permanent part of the lore of the white man's war against the Plains Indians, General George Armstrong Custer. Mounted on a horse in battlefield repose, the defiant gaze of a man who lived and died by the sword looks to the north. Behind the statue is a parking area and small riverside park with a footbridge and nice view of the river.

From the park, Monroe Street crosses the River Raisin and a left on First Street leads to Loranger Square, a quadrant of history laid out in 1817. Buildings in this New England-style square include the 1848 First Presbyterian Church and the 1880 Monroe County Courthouse with its ornate clock tower. An historical marker in the northwest quad tells of the town whipping post that was once here. Public whippings were not common to the Midwest but were used by early, New England settlers here before being abolished in 1835.

From the square, a brief jog north on Washington Street leads to an historic business district on East Front Street. Buildings along here date to the 1850's. Monroe is also home to many historic homes in the near downtown area and an Historic Walking Tour brochure is available at the Monroe County Historical Museum at Monroe and Second streets.

From downtown, Monroe Street north crosses back over the River Raisin. A right on East Elm Avenue leads east to the intersection of North Dixie Highway and left. On the left a short distance down North Dixie Highway is a park and the Vietnam Veterans Memorial. Mounted in the air on a stand in a garden is a battle-scarred Huey Helicopter, frozen in time, its rotor rocking gently in the wind this day. A plaque notes "...the intent of this Vietnam Veterans Memorial site is not to glorify the war but to honor the men and women who courageously served their country..."

Both the museum and River Raisin Battlefield Visitor Center are open seven days a week in summer with limited winter hours. Monroe also hosts Old Frenchtown Days in late August. For more information, call the Monroe County Convention and Visitors Bureau at 800-472-3011 or 313-457-1030.

North Dixie Highway continues north crossing over I-75 to Sterling State Park, a place of broad lawns, sand beach, and quiet lagoon-side picnicking. Hundreds of Canada geese linger and feed here this chilly day as a lone fisherwoman, peering out through the hood of her parka, waits patiently on a rock. Early French settlers, awed by the tremendous flights of waterfowl passing in spring and fall, gathered here to hunt and spear sturgeon.

Sterling State Park has 288 campsites, some with electrical hookups, boat rental, and showers/flush toilets. For more information, call the park at 313-289-2715.

Dixie Highway continues north through the towns of Detroit Beach and Woodland Beach and beyond the cooling towers of the third of three nuclear plants on the lake. It then slants inland to ford Swan Creek over a bridge in the town of Oldport. Aged willows, some broken by storms, grip the banks of the creek here amidst the familiar autumn smell of burning leaves, the smoke lingering over the water.

North of town, Dixie Highway leaves to the left and U.S. Turnpike Road continues along the lake through the low brush of the Point Mouillee State Game Area. The crack of a hunter's rifle echoes through the trees. Where a bridge crosses Mouillee Creek, Riverfront Park gives a nice view of the creek as it widens into a broad body of water and flows into Lake Erie.

The road's name changes to Jefferson Road and moves on to Lake Erie Metropark, a 1,600 acre spread similar to Sterling State Park with a large pool, biking trails, three miles of beach, and the Marshland Museum and Nature Center. Irregular V formations of Canada geese, one arm longer than the other, fly southward overhead passing over a flock of their honking white cousins stopped to feed offshore, geese that far outnumber the few visitors here this day. The mouth of the Detroit River where this journey began on the far bank in October's autumn glow can be seen from the shore.

Clouds are moving in from the west, dulling a tired sun's warmth and within a day will bring some early snow and the season's first hard freeze. Five long months will pass before the songs of spring call man and nature from their winter retreats. Indian Summer is over. It's time to go home.

Out of the Northland sombre weirds are calling;
A shadow falleth southward day by day;
Sad summer's arms grow cold; his fire is falling;
His feet draw back to give the stern one way.
It is the voice and shadow of the slayer,

Slayer of loves, sweet world, slayer of dreams;
Make sad thy voice with sobre plaint and prayer;
Make gray the woods, and darken all the streams.
Black grows the river, blacker drifts the eddy;
The sky is gray; the woods are cold below;
O make thy bosom and thy sad lips ready
For the cold kisses of the folding snow.

Archibald Lampman, *The Coming of Winter*

Appendix:

GENERAL TRAVEL INFORMATION

Ontario Side

Major Parks

On the Ontario shore eight of the nine Ontario Provincial Parks charge admission fee for day-use, the exception being John Pearce Provincial Park which has limited facilities. The Conservation Areas, which are parks operated by regional authorities, also generally charge for admission, particularly if they offer swimming. Point Pelee National Park charges an admission fee as well. The beaches and parks operated by the various small towns along the north shore are generally free.

Lodging

Motel facilities on the north shore between the cities of Leamington on east to Port Colborne are minimal. There's an inn in Port Stanley and a sizable motel in Port Dover and scattered bed and breakfasts. If staying overnight between these two points, travel inland to St. Thomas, Tillsonburg, or Simcoe may be necessary. Plenty of information on lodging including bed and breakfast guides is available at Ontario's fine Travel Information Centers located just over the Ambassador Bridge in Windsor and the Peace Bridge in Fort Erie.

American Side

Major Parks

The two state parks in New York on the lake charge a day-use fee. There is no charge for day-use at Presque Isle State

Park in Pennsylvania or the seven state parks on Lake Erie in Ohio. Sterling State Park in Michigan charges for day-use.

Lodging

As the American side of Lake Erie is much more heavily populated, lodging is much more easily found either in the towns and cities on the lake or along the interstate highways that run parallel to the lake shore.

Additional Travel Information—Phone Numbers

In addition to the phone numbers of the various tourist information centers and visitors bureaus listed in the text, provincial and state operated centers are more than happy to send maps, travel, lodging information, etc. if you call and request such. 1-800-ONTARIO (Ontario); 1-800-CALL-NYS (New York); 1-800-VISIT-PA (Pennsylvania); 1-800-BUCKEYE (Ohio) and 1-800-5432-YES (Michigan).

Border Crossing

If crossing the U.S. or Canadian border for the first time be aware that you do have to stop and answer a few questions from customs agents. These include questions regarding residency and citizenship, length of visit if leaving the country or length of intended stay if entering, luggage, items you purchased and are bringing back with you, and amount of alcohol in the car. Both countries limit the amount of alcohol that can be transported over the border so it's wise to bring only a minimal amount and make any additional purchases once across. Ontario has limits on the amount of cigarettes that travelers can bring into the country. As taxes on tobacco are sharply higher there, cigarette smuggling into Canada has been a problem. For more detailed information call the Ontario travel number. If transporting children be sure to have identification or documentation for them as agents are always on the lookout for child snatching cases.

Bear in mind that, like any international border, customs agents on both sides have the right to search your car and person although this is a rare event. The author has crossed the U.S./Ontario border over 100 times and has been searched only once. That was at a remote crossing in northern Minnesota by U.S. personnel who appeared to be training some young agents.

Currency Exchange

Currency can be exchanged in Ontario at the convenient currency exchange windows at the Ontario Travel Information Centers. The exchange rate given is a couple of points below the official exchange rate which is how the service pays for itself. Banks will exchange currency of course but most charge a small fee for this service.

Retailers in Ontario are under no obligation to offer favorable exchange for the American dollar which at times is worth as much as $1.40 Canadian. Most do offer some exchange but at five to 20% below the official rate. The full exchange rate can be gained by using credit cards both for purchases and for cash advances at banks.

Tips for U.S. travelers to Ontario

U.S. travelers to Ontario should be aware that possession of handguns is illegal in Canada. Also there is an 8% G.S.T. tax (goods and services tax) that is rebatable on lodging and certain hard goods to foreign visitors. The rebate can be obtained in person at the Ontario Travel Information Centers at the border crossings or by mail. For more information, inquire at a Travel Information Center.

U.S. travelers to Ontario seeking to quench their thirst should be aware that all over-the-counter alcohol is sold through government operated stores which are closed on Sundays and holidays. Some beer stores have hours on Sundays preceding a Monday holiday.

On the matter of holidays, Ontario celebrates Christmas, New Years Day, Labor Day, and Veterans Day (Remembrance Day) on the same days as the U.S. The other legal holidays are Easter Monday (day after Easter), Victoria Day (third Monday in May), Canada Day (July 1), Civic Day (first Monday in August); Thanksgiving Day (second Monday in October); and Boxing Day (December 26).

Tips for Canadian Travelers to the United States.

If crossing via the bridge or tunnel at Detroit or the bridge at Buffalo there are, unfortunately, no tourist information centers waiting on the other side. State-operated tourist information centers in the U.S. tend to be located on interstate highways near state borders.

While regulations vary in the four Lake Erie states, generally speaking beer and wine is sold over-the-counter daily including Sundays and holidays. Liquor sales may be restricted on Sundays and holidays.

The U.S. celebrates Christmas, New Years Day, Labor Day, and Remembrance Day (Veterans Day) on the same days as Ontario. The other legal holidays are Martin Luther King Day (third Monday in January); Presidents Day (third Monday in February); Memorial Day (fourth Monday in May); Independence Day (July 4th); Columbus Day (second Monday in October); and Thanksgiving Day (fourth Thursday in November).

Lake Erie Fishing

Lake Erie is one of the great freshwater fishing lakes in North America. Its waters produce more fish than the other four Great lakes combined. The lake is divided into three general areas; the western, central, and eastern basins.

The western basin stretches from the Michigan shore to an approximate line from Sandusky, Ohio across to Point Pelee Ontario. The large central basin ranges from the Sandusky/ Point Pelee boundary to a line roughly from Erie, Pa. across to Long Point, Ontario. The eastern basin runs from the Erie/ Long Point line to Buffalo. The lake deepens as it moves from west to east and reaches its maximum depth of 210 feet off the tip of the Long Point peninsula about midway between the Ontario and U.S. shore.

The return of health to Lake Erie has made it an enormously popular fishing lake with walleye being taken by the millions. However smallmouth bass and yellow perch remain very popular panfish and the stocking in recent years of chinook and coho salmon and steelhead and rainbow trout have only added to Lake Erie's seafood bill of fare. In addition so called "trash fish," such as carp, bullhead, and sheepshead that even the pollution of the 1960's could not kill off, remain in the lake in great numbers.

However it is the walleye which is the undisputed champion of the Lake Erie fishing world. In the mid-1980's the walleye population in Lake Erie exploded to roughly 120 million. This was due to a variety of factors including a lack of other fish species competing for food. Since then it has stabilized at around 50 million, still a tremendous number.

Walleye activity begins in earnest in early spring in the shallow waters of the western basin which warm first. Here the walleye spawn both in the shoals and sandy bottom of the lake and, in large numbers, up the Maumee and Sandusky Rivers. In early April the banks of these two rivers are frequently lined with anglers standing nearly shoulder-to-shoulder.

As the lake warms from west to east, so follow schools of walleye and by end of June they've spread through the central basin and are moving into the eastern. And it is in the deep waters of the eastern basin where the angler is more likely to find trophy size walleye, ten plus pounds, as well as the species of trout and salmon that call Lake Erie home.

The lazy days of summer finds good fishing around and across the lake and thousands of lines are cast daily from private boats, charters, piers, and breakwalls. As summer cools into fall, the walleye drift back toward the western basin and the perch move toward shallower waters near the shore.

As fall becomes winter the lake begins to freeze and in a cold year will ice over completely. This brings out the ice fishermen and their varied huts and shanties, particularly in bays and harbors around the lake and in the open ice of the western basin where the majority of the lake's walleye spend the winter. And through augured holes in the ice many a fine specimen of walleye and perch are pulled.

But the wind, southerly or easterly in particular, can turn a small crack in the ice into a chasm. And many an unwary western basin fisherman over the years has been deeply chagrined to find himself on a slow drift toward Ontario on an ice floe raft, a dangerous place to be in freezing waters. Then its Coast Guard and Sheriff Department helicopters to the rescue for an expensive, and for the angler, embarrassing, deliverance.

Lake Erie is a lake for all seasons. But for those who love to fish it there are some clouds on the horizon. There have been slight declines in the 1990's in the walleye population and a more serious decline in the numbers of perch.

Experts debate the reasons as to why but one factor is increasingly clear. The little zebra mussel, which first invaded the Great Lakes around 1985 probably via an ocean freighter's ballast discharge, is making a big impact. Each mussel can filter over a quart of water per day and, as a result, the lake's water is clearer than it has been in decades.

However also filtered out by the millions of mussels is phytoplankton, the base of the lake's foodchain. In addition the new clarity of the water is allowing sunlight to reach previously unreachable depths, thus preventing growth of sun-sensitive plants.

One way to increase the growth of phytoplankton and aquatic vegetation is to increase the amount of the nutrient phosphorous in the lake. It was excessive phosphorous-primarily from laundry detergents and human waste-that led to explosive growths of algae that had nearly choked Lake Erie to death by the mid-1960's. Its release by sewage treatment plants was subsequently tightly regulated, which was a major factor in Lake Erie's comeback.

Now proposals are being debated to increase the amount of phosphorous discharged into the lake in the early spring when the mussels are generally dormant. Ideally this would spur aquatic food growth on which spawning fish could feed, a seemingly simple solution.

However complex problems rarely have simple answers. And, as the years roll on, more fundamental changes to Lake Erie brought by mankind's presence are likely to be seen.

Lake Erie Islands

The western basin of Lake Erie is home to a 20 island archipelago ranging from uninhabited rocky outcrops to islands set aside as bird sanctuaries to isles with communities and year 'round residents. The islands are believed to be the remnants of a rock bridge that once stretched across the lake. Three of the four islands open to the public are in U.S. waters.

Kelley's Island lies 3.5 miles north of the Marblehead Peninsula and is the largest of the U.S. islands. Two brothers named Kelley from Cleveland purchased the island in the 1830's and built an elegant mansion that stands today. The mansion rents rooms in the summer and is open for tours.

The glaciers that helped create Lake Erie left their calling card on Kelley's Island in the form of 15-foot deep limestone glacial grooves considered to be the largest in the world. More stony island history can be seen at the Inscription Rock State Memorial where the Eriez Indians carved pictographs nearly 400 years ago.

The south side of the island has a downtown with shops and restaurants while the north side is home to Kelley's Island State Park, with camping and a fine sand beach.

Kelley's is considered to be the most unspoiled of the U.S. islands and vehicular traffic is limited. Visitors to the island can travel by golf cart or bicycle which are available for rent.

South Bass Island lies 3.5 miles north of the tip of the peninsula known as Catawba Island and is the most visited of the U.S. islands. The north shore of the island is home to the village of Put-in-Bay and its large, natural harbor that swells with a variety of boats and watercraft on warm summer weekends. Many a ship's captain "put in the bay" when weather threatened over the years, thus the village's name. It was from this scenic harbor that Commodore Perry sailed his fleet on September 10, 1813 to meet the British in the Battle of Lake Erie. One of the island's most popular attractions is the 352-foot tall Perry's Victory and International Peace Memorial. The view from the observation deck of this fluted pink granite column on a clear day is stunning.

Downtown Put-in-Bay exudes a turn-of-the-century charm and is home to numerous bars, restaurants, shops, and other attractions. One of those attractions is Kimberly's Carousel, built in 1917, where children can whirl on wooden horses while organ music plays. A large town park on the waterfront provides relaxation, picnicking under tall shade trees, and public restrooms with showers. And the Lake Erie Islands Historical

Society Museum downtown records the rich history of South Bass Island.

A half-mile south of downtown on Catawba Avenue is Heineman's Winery, owned by the same family for over 100 years. A tour includes a stop at Crystal Cave, 40 feet directly below the winery. The cave is the largest geode in the world. Across the street lies Perry Cave, named for the Commodore, and purportedly used by him to store gunpowder and later to house British prisoners of war.

Where Catawba Avenue ends lies South Bass Island State Park with camping and a public beach. And, like Kelleys Island, South Bass can be toured on foot, via rented bicycle or golf cart, or tour train.

Middle Bass Island lies a good stone's throw north of South Bass. Early French explorers originally named it *Isle de Fleurs,* or "the floral island," for its numerous wildflowers. In 1856 a German count bought the island and the Duetschlanders that followed him established vineyards. A result of all this grape growing is the Lonz Winery.

An eclectic mix of brick, stone, and wood, the winery building looks like a medieval castle where it rises into the sky on the south shore of Middle Bass. Visitors can enjoy food and wine on stone porches while taking in a fine view of Lake Erie. Underneath, cavernous cellars carved out of solid limestone house great wooden wine casks.

The floral island still retains its quiet beauty with only a smattering of automobiles and no public transportation. Unlike Kelley's and South Bass there is no town or public parkland here, only a general store. For those wanting to explore the island there are roads for walking and in the northeast part of the island lies marshland and a sandy beach.

Pelee Island, by far the largest of the Lake Erie islands, lies a few miles north of the International Boundary Line in Ontario waters. It is Canada's southernmost land mass and, with the moderating waters of Lake Erie, lays claim to Canada's longest growing season. The isle was the site of Fenians Raid or The Battle of the Ice in 1838.

The island was captured in March of that year during the Patriots Rebellion by a force of 450 Canadian rebels and their

American sympathizers who crossed the frozen lake from Ohio. Before long, British regulars from Fort Malden aided by Canadian militia sent the rebels scurrying back cross the ice but not before a brief skirmish during which ten rebels were killed.

The bulk of the rebel force escaped to Sandusky where they were disarmed and dispersed by the Ohio Militia. The event marked the last major clash of the Patriots Rebellion and the last time Canadian and American forces crossed swords.

In subsequent years the rich soil of the island produced tobacco, corn, soybeans, and grapes. Pelee is now home to the Pelee Island Winery with its 500 acres of vineyards and Wine Pavilion for tasting and tours. Visitors to the Pavilion can barbecue their own lunch as the winery sells meat and provides gas grills with which to cook it.

Other points of interest include the ruins of the Vin Villa Winery built in 1865 and the old Pelee Island Lighthouse built in 1834. The island is also home to two nature reserves with marked trails; the Lighthouse Point Nature Reserve on its northern tip and the Fish Point Nature Reserve on its southern tip.

Time has not changed Pelee Island much and it remains a quiet and rural enclave. With over 50 miles of mostly unpaved roads there's plenty of opportunity to explore via bicycle or auto.

Those planning overnight stays on any of the islands during the summer months should make reservations well in advance. Lodging and ferry information for Middle and South Bass Island can be obtained by calling the Ottawa County Visitors Bureau at 800-441-1271. Kelley's Island information can be obtained by calling the Sandusky/Erie County Convention and Visitors Bureau at 800-255-ERIE.

Information on Pelee Island ferries departing from the U.S. can be obtained by calling the Sandusky/Erie County number. Information on Pelee Island ferries departing from Ontario can be obtained by calling 800-661-2220. Pelee Island travel information can be obtained by writing to Public Relations, Pelee Island, Ontario, NOR 1MO.

INDEX:

About the Author:

Jim Mollenkopf is a free-lance writer and photographer from Toledo, Ohio, who has camped and travelled extensively in the Great Lakes area over the years. He was a social worker for 18 years, then a reporter for *The Review Times* newspaper in Fostoria, Ohio.

This is his first book.